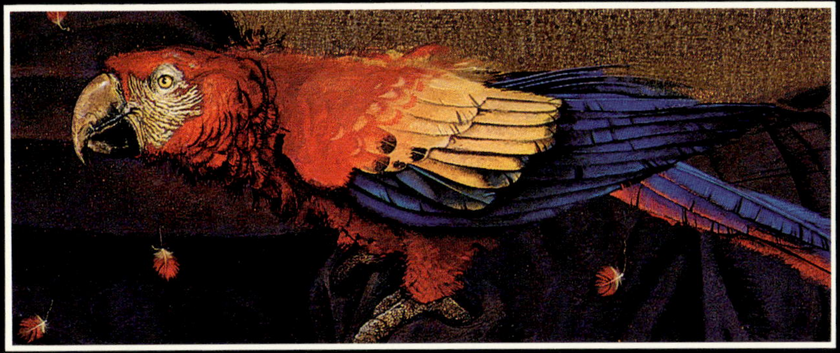

PLETKA

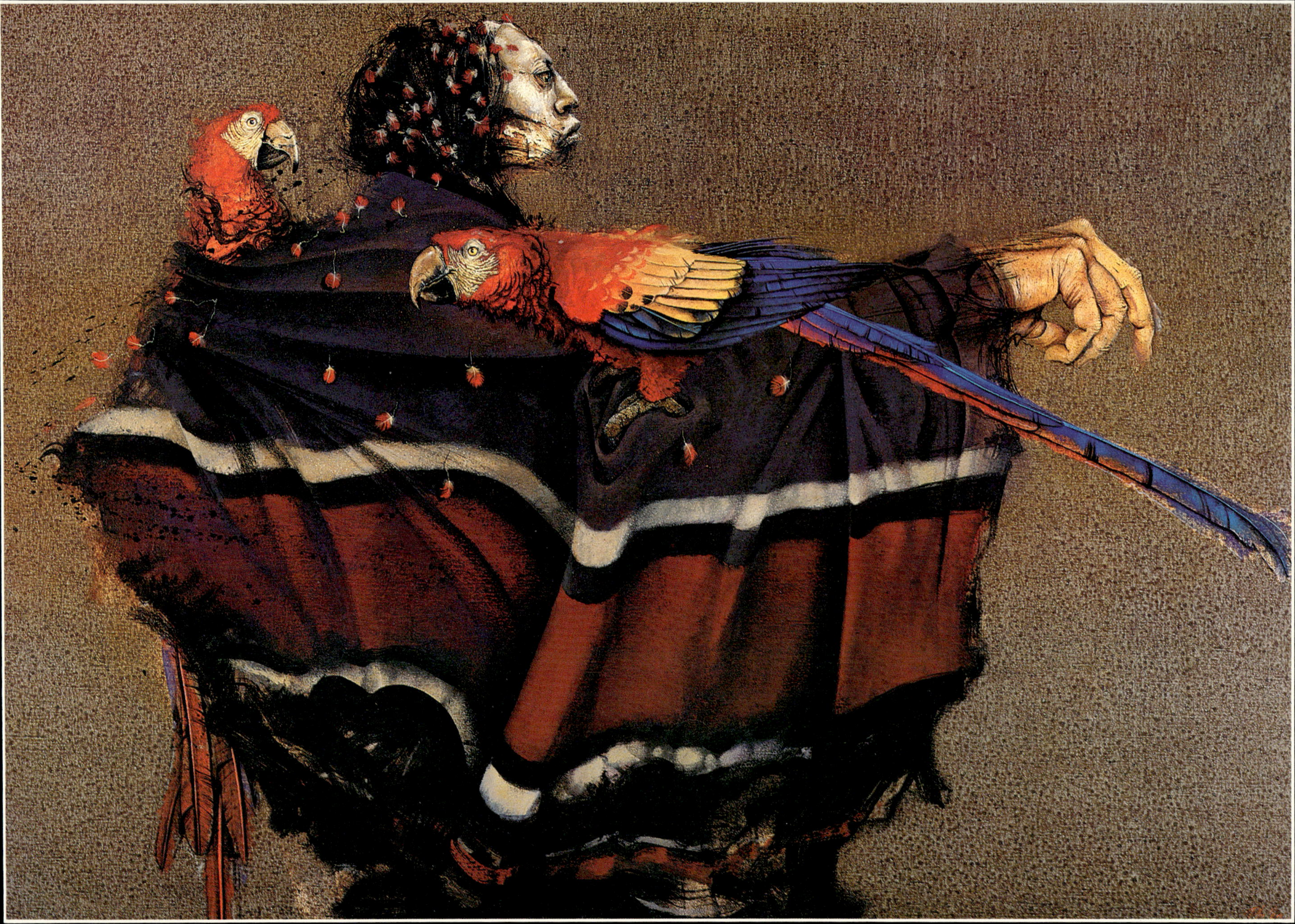

PLETKA

INTRODUCTION BY EVAN MAURER

NORTHLAND PRESS • FLAGSTAFF, ARIZONA

Permission has been granted to Northland Press by Jack O'Grady Galleries, Chicago, Illinois, to reproduce the art on pp. 45, 50, and 52; by The Art Institute of Chicago to reproduce the art on p. 16; by the Center for Western Studies, Joslyn Art Museum, Omaha, Nebraska, to reproduce the art on p. 34; and by Editions Gallimard, Paris, France, to use the quotation on p. 1.

FIRST PRINTING
ISBN 0-87358-309-4 Cloth Edition
ISBN 0-87358-311-6 Limited Edition
Library of Congress Catalog Card Number 82-81691
Composed and Printed in the United States of America

IN MEMORY OF

LOUIS MCLANE

June 23, 1935–January 15, 1981

Contents

PLETKA

To Ruth B. Johnston
Warmest Regards
Paul

Introduction

"I believe that men will long feel the need to retrace to its true source the magical river that flows from their eyes, bathing with the same light and the same hallucinatory shadow those things that are and those things that are not."

André Breton

André Breton's poetic evocation of the surrealist artist describes the quest of many who have sought to express the spiritual basis of life through visual means. The work of Paul Pletka is very much a part of this symbolic and visionary tradition and stands as an eloquent record of his personal pursuit of this enigmatic goal. The magic realism of his paintings and their elemental themes of life and death, growth and decay are inspired by the mystic Native American cultures of the Plains, the Pueblos, and the Penitentes of the Southwest. Whatever the sources of his imagery, however, the technical, visual, and spiritual qualities of his work have many affinities to European and American artists of the past whose different subject matter portrayed a similarly intense world view.

Pletka has studied the work of many artists and has adapted their lessons into his own creative language. For many years he has been attracted by the precise technique and emotional intensity of northern Renaissance artists such as Rogier van der Weyden and Hieronymus Bosch; but it is perhaps with the work of Matthias Grünewald, a German painter of the sixteenth-century whom he much admires, that Pletka's own paintings have the closest affinities. Grünewald's image of the wracked and decaying body of Christ in the Crucifixion panel of his famous Isenheim Altarpiece inspired the nineteenth-century symbolist writer J. K. Huysmans to describe this work in terms that recall Pletka's visualizations of spirituality and death: "Never before had naturalism transfigured itself by such a conception and execution. Never before had a painter so charnelly envisaged divinity nor so brutally dipped his brush into the wounds and running sores and bleeding nail holes of the Saviour. . . . In this canvas was revealed the masterpiece of an art obeying the unopposable urge to render the tangible and the invisible, to make manifest the crying impurity of the flesh, and to make sublime the infinite distress of the soul."

Pletka's involvement with intense and often macabre subject matter is also reminiscent of the work of Francis Bacon and Ivan Albright, two twentieth-century artists famous for their powerful figurative imagery. The twisted agony of Bacon's popes and cardinals, their compositional isolation in the center of the canvas, and their sense of scale are influences that Paul Pletka freely acknowledges. But an even closer visual relationship can be seen in the work of Albright, an American whose paintings on the theme of human experience and suffering are executed with extraordinarily rich and detailed surfaces. As with Albright's representation of precipitous entropy in his painting, *The Picture of Dorian Gray,* Pletka's technique relies on the careful building up of layers of drawing and color glazes. The impact of the detail is further heightened by Pletka's isolation of the main images against comparatively plain backgrounds, a device that also has the effect of creating a timeless universal setting.

Like many artists of the nineteenth and twentieth centuries, Pletka represents the spiritual harmony of the world through personal representations based on so-called primitive cultures. The effectiveness of his Native American imagery is directly related to his study of and profound feeling for these cultures and the objects they produced. This involvement is enriched by his recognition of the inherent power of the object as a creative metaphor expressing man's need to transcend the world of physical reality by invoking a mythic and eternal state. Through expressive manipulation, his bold figures of Plains warriors and Ghost Dance participants produce an active tension between the viewer's visual attraction to the detailed rendering of body, object and costume, and the emotional impact of the painting as a whole. Pletka delights in representing the individual texture and surface quality of Indian sacred objects and takes great care to portray the essential nature of the materials used. Delicate feathers are contrasted to painted leather; multi-colored glass beads are isolated against the warm, somber tones of the earth; soft fur and polished horn are set against skies which vary from soft blues to menacing blacks. The same sensitive attention is given to the depiction of the people as well, and again Pletka entices the viewer with carefully wrought and expressive incongruities. The details of surface appearances are captured with convincing accuracy, yet individual elements of the figures are distorted into exaggerated proportions, most often emphasizing the hands and the head. Pletka's depiction of the Indians' painted faces is an especially powerful element in his work. His realistic rendering of pigments on skin is a technical *tour de force* given transformative power by his conception of the painted face as a mask which symbolizes the concentration of the individual's ability to simultaneously tap his inner sources of strength and to identify himself with the larger whole of which he is a part. The belief that the individual shares a motivating spiritual force with all other manifestations of nature is central to Native American philosophy. Paul Pletka's creations are reflective of his personal struggle to evoke this attitude through his art.

Ultimately, the impact of Pletka's work derives from the primacy of spiritual concerns throughout all the stages of the painting's development. He conceptualizes the theme of each picture and then seeks the objects and images that will best express that fundamental idea. Through this process, the representational imagery serves to suggest the correspondences that exist between the physical forms and the spiritual forces they embody and imply. The haunting attraction of Paul Pletka's art results from the sincerity of his feelings and beliefs, as well as from his ability to convey the essence of both emotion and philosophy through the magic of the visual image. His path is not an easy one, but the fruits of his journey have been works of compelling beauty and mystery.

E.M.

P. 1. André Breton, *Surrealism and Painting,* translated by Simon Watson Taylor, New York, Harper and Row, Publishers, Paris, © Editions Gallimard, 1965, p. 7.

J. K. Huysmans, *Là-Bas,* translated by Keene Wallace, New York, Dover Publications, Inc., 1972, p. 14–15.

Profile

I do not believe in art which has not forced its way forward from man's need to open his heart. Art is one's life blood.

EDVARD MUNCH

Paul Pletka's first monumental portrait of an Indian did not elicit the kind of gushing praise his paintings receive today. In fact, the inaugural work earned him a sharp scolding and a long sit in the corner. The canvas was a white sheet from his mother's linen closet. The medium was crayon, a stubborn substance impervious to laundry detergent. The artist was six years old.

Throughout his childhood Pletka drew Indians. There was little else that occupied his fantasies, demanded his every free hour, and devoured his energies. For better or worse, William Paul Pletka Johnson seemed destined to be a painter.

Born in San Diego in 1946, Paul was the first child of Anna Marie Pletka and Howard Paul Johnson. By the time their daughter, Jan Marie, was born five years later, their son was showing all indications of being an artistic prodigy, as well as a novice historian. Howard Johnson, now retired after thirty-seven years as a glazier, remembers Pletka's earliest interests in Indians and art: "The family still has a piece of crayon work, a portrait of an Indian, that Paul did when he was about four years old. That's when I first noticed his talent. He got his fascination with Indians from me. My interest began about the time I was ten or twelve; Paul's started when he was five. The first time he saw my small collection of arrowheads, he was hooked. Periodically, he would ask me to bring him the arrowheads so he could look through them. His curiosity was extraordinary. Usually a youngster will be interested in something for a little while, then it suddenly becomes a dead issue. Paul stuck it out, with both his artwork and his Indian interest."

Pletka's mother, now Anna Hosier, notes, "He was still young enough to be in the high chair when I bought him his first coloring book. He would sit there quietly coloring, doing a beautiful job. He must have been about three years old. Later, after he began school, I remember that his kindergarten teacher called me to school for a conference. She said, 'I don't know if you realize this, but your boy has great artistic ability.' I began to wonder then if he might not have a future in art. I still have drawings from that period."

In retrospect, Pletka feels that the case for his early genius might be a bit overdrawn. He is, however, very outspoken about the positive relationship with his parents. "Most of the artists I've known feel they had to struggle against the odds of parents who thought they should pursue a more lucrative profession. I, on the other hand, always had the understanding and support of my parents. My father's knowledge of Indian traditions was very significant in my early development."

When he was not making Indian costumes or drawing Indian pictures, Pletka was reading books about Indian lore and history. "From the time I was old enough to think," he says, "I was reading about Indians. My father's interest was contagious. The moment he introduced me to his world of Indian artifacts, I was utterly, desperately fascinated. The first time he mentioned something about an Indian feather, I was a goner. He dabbled in taxidermy, which impressed me. So I began collecting things early. I've always been object-oriented and visually attuned."

Pletka rarely misbehaved, and although he engaged in typical childhood games and sports, his parents remember him as a serious, reserved adolescent whose primary interest was Indians and art. He drew with crayons, pencils, and pastels constantly. Other children his age found toy trucks and balsa airplanes under the Christmas tree. Pletka, to his delight, found easels and watercolor sets. Allowance money went for Indian costume kits bought from mail order firms in New York. Pletka studied and practiced Indian dance steps to a point of proficiency that allowed him a solo performance in the annual Pacific Beach parade.

Because of a demonstrable photographic memory, Pletka seldom needed to bring his school books home. Besides, he found grade school lessons and tests insipid compared to his independent research of Indians.

He was eleven years old when the family moved to Grand Junction, Colorado. His father, a Wyoming native reared in Iowa, had grown tired of southern California and willingly took a drastic pay cut to relocate in a rural environment more conducive to hunting, fishing, and exploring. Howard Johnson remembers the move with one major regret: "When I left California, I had a big cardboard box full of Paul's drawings. There was no room to store it, so I threw it away."

In Colorado, Pletka's intrigue with Indians grew. He joined an Indian dance group, composed primarily of Anglo youths, but directed and choreographed by an Hidatsa Indian. Throughout junior high school, he continued drawing and reading with the enthusiastic support of his parents. As a teenager, Pletka discovered King Tutankhamen and, for a few years, became obsessed by Egyptology. "Strange Egyptian symbolism crept into my work," he says. "My appetite for knowledge was boundless and everything was so interesting I found it impossible to narrow my focus. I consumed a lot of information but couldn't make sense of it. One day I'd be reading about the Lewis and Clark Expedition, and the next day I'd have my nose in the *Book of the Dead*. I studied Egyptian hieroglyphics for a long time."

In high school, Pletka was easily distracted. He

found it extremely difficult to concentrate on prescribed academic exercise. With a smile he remembers when his physics teacher told him, "I'll pass you if you promise never to take a physics or chemistry course in college." He is grateful for the encouragement of his English teacher. "I drew and painted my way through class. The teacher knew I was hopeless, so he let me focus my attention on something I did well." Paul's mother was in agreement with his artistic aspirations, but his father had reservations. "I was worried, because artists were a dime a dozen," Pletka's father says. "But he was *so* determined." While his peers danced to Elvis records and worked to raise money for convertibles, Pletka withdrew into his cubbyhole of sketch pads.

"I was a very introspective child, very antisocial and not outgoing at all," he admits. "I had no social life. None. All my energies were invested in painting or drawing. I wasn't completely out of touch with the times, however. I remember how much I admired John Lennon. I began to adopt eccentric dress and the manner that went with it. I saw myself as a restrained but earnest rebel."

When Pletka wasn't drawing, he was hunting for artifacts. He worked with his father at the glass warehouse during summer months; on weekends the pair would search for arrowheads on the outskirts of town. The outings were enjoyable, but not nearly as exciting as the family jaunts to southeastern Utah. The annual trips were to become a potent influence in Pletka's work.

"If anything in my past has influenced my work," he says, "it's those visits to Utah, specifically the beautiful country around Blanding and Monticello. I was fascinated by the multitude of geological forms and the clean air. I was intrigued by the history of the region, the oldness of it, both in terms of geology and anthropology. I felt the texture and flow of the environment and was in love with those wonderful names—Dead Man's Canyon, Mummy Canyon, Disappointment. These fabulous, romantic places were wild and relatively unexplored. On these trips, I learned to observe. I began to watch birds, to see what made them function. I became conscious of how they flew and how they were designed. Ravens are enchanting when they glide through canyons on the updrafts and make their haunting cry.

"I began to see trees and rock formations as sculpture. The huge mesas and plunging canyons had a fundamental influence later when I approached the human figure. The enormity of the western landscape, which was so difficult to capture, was easier to incorporate into expansive, directional figures. Through those figures, I was able to say what I felt for the landscape.

"In 1963, my father and I were driving in a jeep somewhere east of Blanding. We found a couple of bad ruts, tracks through a thick piñon and juniper forest. We followed them and came upon a clearing apparently caused by fire some years earlier. There was a very thick secondary growth, about two feet high, of wheat grass. And in this sea of grass were the skeletons of numerous burned junipers and piñons, whitened, sun-bleached affairs, lots of them. There was a hazy, dull sun.

"I was immediately struck by the fact that perched in these trees were about three dozen ravens, sunning themselves. Some had their wings spread. They were all chattering back and forth. The impact on me was incredible. I realized this was an experience of real, deep magic. It lasted maybe thirty seconds, and then we were gone, heading north out of the area. My immediate reaction was to go home and set this impression on paper or canvas or something. But I realized I couldn't. It was beyond my abilities and always would be. It was the ultimate Morris Graves painting, but more magical, more encompassing. It possessed a spiritual quality. Even now, when I see a single raven, the ceremony of ravens in the dead trees goes careening through my mind and gives me a sense of joy. It was magic, and I knew I could never recreate it, but I've always tried to include pieces of that experience in my paintings.

"I'm still drawn to that region of Utah. I can feel the antiquity when I'm there. It sounds crazy, but I can feel the souls of the ancient people. I can almost hear them padding across that soft red earth. Whenever I return there, I am somehow nourished. It's my fondest wish to someday have a studio lost in the piñon forests east of Blanding."

Another taproot—acclaim—was feeding Pletka's determination. He won several prizes in high school art contests, as well as a prestigious award for an illustration he submitted to *Seventeen* magazine, which published the entry. He also secured a national scholarship. "The awards and recognition spurred me," Pletka says, "and I discovered I could sell readily. I sold drawings to neighbors, teachers, strangers. It was a pleasing experience, even though it didn't have much to do with creating art."

In 1964, Pletka graduated from Grand Junction High School. He began his college career with a scholarship to Arizona State University, returning to Grand Junction in 1965, where he enrolled in Mesa College. He transferred to Colorado State University in 1967 and discovered two professors who helped him further hone his talents. He says, "One of them was LeRoy Twarogowski, a product of the Chicago Art Institute. He taught me drawing techniques and helped me sharpen my raw abilities. The other was Jack Orman, from the University of Iowa, whose presence at Colorado State was the motivating influence in my transfer. He had a lot of strength and discipline. I was vastly improved by his teaching of both printmaking and proper drawing technique. He was an exceptionally good professor."

Orman remembers Pletka as an industrious, aggressive student who quickly mastered lithography. "I enjoyed teaching him very much," Orman says. "He was bright, had an interesting outlook on life, and was seriously involved with his art. He was rather quiet and introspective, not the usual free-flowing college student. He was more immersed in his work than most, and in the sense of his subject matter, very genuine. I thought his work was considerably better than a lot of western-oriented art in the modern period, because Pletka's art was less sentimental. It was direct."

Pletka remembers these two professors as highlights in what was otherwise a rather non-productive college career. Looking back, he comments, "I now understand that the disappointment was partially my own fault. I erroneously expected that a system geared to produce results of a uniform quality would help me become, in some way, unique.

"Rauchenberg and Rivers, masters of the sixties, provided the model for many of the students, but my self-esteem, or ego, wouldn't let me become a clone.

"I agonized over my inability to conform to the

popular campus wisdom and dogma—so much so that after leaving school, I spent several years in a state of semi-paralysis, unable to reconcile my natural proclivities with what the university told me was correct. I produced very little, although this was partially because of a full-time museum job; what was accomplished was fragmented and confused.

"When this two-year period of inertia ended, I shed the excess baggage of art school dogma and came to the realization that my work must be honest, that I could and should exploit my natural drawing ability."

Pletka was married in 1968, but home life could not compare to the excitement he found in the studio, where he was embarking on a passionate relationship with paint. Pletka had never taken a painting course. His focus in college had been printmaking. Consequently, he refined his techniques through experimentation.

In 1969, this budding career was interrupted by a brief stint with the National Guard. From January to May, he took basic training and Advanced Individual Training at Fort Ord, California, an experience he despised. He found that being forced to cut his hair and the separation from his studio were the most painful parts of the ordeal.

Fulfilling his obligation to the U.S. Government and free again to pursue painting, Pletka was perplexed and slightly disoriented. College had left him disenchanted, and while he felt confidence in his skills, he was plagued by fears that his rejection of academic gospel had been too hasty. Those worries abated with the occurrence of a few commercial coups. His first market was in Ouray, Colorado. From there, his works traveled to Taos, New Mexico, where he was represented by a series of well-known galleries. His paintings sold briskly; his self-assurance increased.

"I had finally developed the confidence to work in larger scale," he says. "I think it was in 1972 when I broke the barrier. The main thing that stopped me from doing larger paintings in the first place was the message from the galleries that people couldn't fit them in their homes. Also, I had to get to a point where I could finance the canvas, and I needed the physical space so I could make a bigger mess. When all this fell together, I began my large pictures, and that provided a spark. There was a rush of excitement associated with it, a burst of energy, and then a chain reaction. I started to grow again. I started to think again."

Pletka transferred his painting repertoire to a gallery in Scottsdale in late 1973, a change that produced a halcyon season. Three shows in three years attracted stampedes of buyers eager to own Pletka's mammoth examinations of Indian mysticism. At Pletka's annual exhibition in 1975, an ample collection of new paintings, lithographs, and watercolors sold out within fifteen minutes after the gallery doors were unlocked. Painting diligently in his Grand Junction studio, Pletka could not keep pace with demand—a remarkable achievement for an artist.

On the heels of commercial success in Scottsdale and accolades from a Chicago showing came two setbacks that further reduced his traditionally limited output. First, Pletka was divorced in 1976 after eight years of marriage. Second, after moving to Phoenix that year, he contracted a progressive form of valley fever. The illness so debilitated him that he was intermittently bedridden for a year.

This bleak period was brightened by the entrance of Nancy Benkof, raised in St. Louis and schooled at the University of Denver and the University of Colorado at Boulder. After a year of teaching English abroad, Nancy returned and settled in Phoenix. While working for a gallery there, she met Pletka. "I didn't think much of him," Nancy confesses. "He was tense, always operating in high gear." Time, however, tempered her initial impression, and Nancy became enamored of the fretful, intense painter.

"Meeting Nancy was wonderful," Pletka says. "She is logical and practical. She helped me mature."

Nancy says, "Paul softened me. He taught me to open up. When we met, I was very militant. I had a lot of hard edges. He soothed those tendencies in me."

Another important friendship developed during these Phoenix days with sculptor and jeweler Larry Golsh, an Indian of Pala Mission and Cherokee heritage. The two shared a studio, as well as a philosophy and a number of personality traits. Both were reticent, solemn, devoted to their work, and infatuated with the other's work. "The quality and seriousness of Paul's work impressed me," Golsh says, "and I appreciated how thoroughly he researched his subjects, whether a geographic detail, a costume, a basket, a bird, or a pot. Accuracy was important to him. In sharing a studio, we were very compatible. It seems Paul tended to work in the afternoons and evenings, and I was more a morning person. We had similar habits. I'm not the neatest person when I'm working, but neither is Paul. I like to leave things scattered on my work table. He and I accumulated things and littered them around the studio: furs and feathers and beads and blankets, things for us to stare at and unconsciously get ideas from. Clutter can be creative.

"We didn't communicate much, at least not verbally. We didn't have to. We responded to each other's work and expressed our appreciation without a lot of words, without reinforcing each other's egos. It was simply understood. We've remained close friends, even though we don't see each other often. We don't need a lot of conversation. Five minutes is enough to renew the ties."

The summer of 1977 was a significant one to Pletka. He and Nancy moved to a house and studio in Tesuque, New Mexico, ten miles north of Santa Fe, on top of a broad mesa. On July 9, they were married.

Pletka resumed work immediately and was making good progress when the news of his Scottsdale manager's bankruptcy reached him. It was a severe blow to his career and one that made him question his heretofore *carte blanche* trust of others.

One of his friends recalls how the experience affected Pletka: "Before everything fell apart, Paul had complete faith in the people he worked with. He trusted you until you gave him reason not to. Now he's leery of everyone he meets. No exceptions. He's distant and slow to accept new people into his confidence."

Though initially stunned, Pletka rebounded with surprising swiftness and began painting with new vigor. He restored his career and, after prudent deliberation, became affiliated with new dealers whom he judged to be ethical and sincere. He more closely involved himself in his commercial affairs. These recuperative efforts included a successful New York solo exhibition in April, 1978. Since then,

Pletka has found acclaim and success through shows in Scottsdale, Aspen, and without abatement, New York.

"He's complicated when it comes to his work," Nancy says. "Otherwise, he's fairly easygoing. He loves to sit around and talk with friends. He appreciates down-to-earth people." His placid lifestyle notwithstanding, Pletka is often an anxious person. Nancy adds, "Sometimes Paul seems to work while he's sleeping. He wakes me up at 2:00 in the morning, bolts upright, his heart pounding. 'The world is pouncing on me,' he says, and he launches into a draining self-evaluation, unleashing his fears and frustrations. It's hard on him."

Attribution and Evocation

The most beautiful thing we can experience is the mysterious. It is the source of all true art and science.

ALBERT EINSTEIN

Had Pletka lived in the fifteenth century, he might have found himself among a new wave of painters breaking from the traditions of visual arts touted during the last decades of the Middle Ages. He might have been a student of the Master of Flemalle, believed to have been Robert Campin (ca. 1375–1444), whose *Merode Altarpiece,* with its dramatic depth and spatial consistency, launched a pictorial revolution in Flanders labeled loosely as the Late Gothic period. He might have found himself among the pioneering painters whose innovations laid the foundation of Renaissance art. He would have felt at home.

As it is, Pletka's work exists in stunning dichotomy to contemporary art.

"About ten years ago I made a conscious decision to attempt something different, something that's been out of fashion for almost four hundred years. Maybe I should say 'I sought a revival of an art form.'

"Although there is work of integrity and skill being produced at this time, the modern modes being used don't speak to me. I respond with more excitement to the earlier, more direct work—the post-Gothic masters of pre-Renaissance Europe and social realists and surrealists of mid-twentieth-century America. I'm striving to meld two aims, to create well-executed paintings with a strong visceral quality.

"What I'm doing is interpretive and subjective. A lot of my work relates to time and metamorphism, which to my mind is best exposed through exacting technical passages—techniques akin to those of surrealism and post-Gothic masters. It is this approach that separates my work from contemporary western art."

Pletka has no interest in simply restating the story of the old West, of artistically regurgitating factual information. "I consider that approach to art insincere. Of course, I use facts—such as ethnological material, historical events, and costume detail—not for their own sake, but for a broader purpose."

Distressed by the faddish machinations of the contemporary art field, Pletka has sought solace and inspiration in a more inviting atmosphere—the churning, artistically fertile niche between the late Middle Ages and the blossoming Renaissance: The Roman Catholic Church was losing its iron grip on society; commerce was brisk; art was a passion. Still psychologically influenced by the catastrophic Black Death of 1348, artists of the fifteenth century painted formidable, richly symbolic, painstakingly detailed works that responded to the calamity with one of two viewpoints. One side interpreted the plague as divine punishment and an omen of further devastation if man did not mend his sinful ways. The other viewed the cataclysm as a reminder to relish life's pleasures while they last. Curiously, some painters combined the opposing theories.

Pletka feels a strong kindred spirit with post-Gothic painters, particularly Hieronymus Bosch and Rogier van der Weyden. Bosch was born in the Netherlands around 1450. He married an aristocratic woman in 1478 and died in 1516. Few other details of his life are documented, establishing the Flemish genius as one of history's most enigmatic and diversely interpreted painters. He created astonishingly complex panoramas of fanciful figures engaged in obviously sensual, but not readily decipherable, activities. His *magnum opus* and most inexplicable work is the *Garden of Earthly Delights* triptych at the Prado in Madrid. Pletka's favorite Bosch work is *The Hay-Wain,* an oil triptych painted between 1480 and 1485. Based on a Dutch proverb, "The world is a heap of hay; everyone grabs some while he may," the religious narrative explores fraud and greed.

Rogier van der Weyden (ca. 1400–1464), a Flemish painter who may have been an apprentice of Robert Campin, clearly admired Jan van Eyck (ca. 1380–1441), as does Pletka. Gold dominated the painter's characteristically Gothic palette, and pigment was applied boldly and in undiminished concentrations. Van der Weyden especially influenced the portraiture of the Netherlands in the late fifteenth century.

It was less their proficiency than their pathos that drew Pletka to post-Gothic artists. He says, "I feel an affinity for painters of the post-Gothic period, particularly those who produced pictures in Flanders and Burgundy. The plague had thrown the people of Europe into a panic. There was terrible uncertainty in the air, because nobody knew when and how severely this awful disease would strike again. That triggered all sorts of fluctuations in society, which were reflected in rather aberrant paintings. The period produced wonderful, sensitive pictures. Rogier van der Weyden's *Deposition of Christ,* an altarpiece painted circa 1438 and now hanging in the Prado, is possibly my favorite painting. It embodies everything I strive for in my paintings. It has humanity. It is steeped in history. The colors are rich. It has a tremendous sweep and presence. It has drama. It has all I consider paramount in a picture.

"Hieronymus Bosch, a strange man, considered anomalous even in his day, painted nightmarish pictures that were probably a reaction to insecurities in society. This instability produced a kind of fundamentalist attitude toward religion and included elements of self-flagellation, not unlike what is happening presently in New Mexico and southern Colorado with the Penitentes. I am attracted to the older liturgical paintings by their richness and by the obvious care and love that was put into producing them."

Art buffs trained to appreciate only a painting's

superficial embroidery may never grasp the mystic tenor of Pletka's work. Some viewers may gradually discover the artist's bearing; few seize it instantly. One of Pletka's followers comments, "When I began studying Pletka's work, I was very impressed with the fact that there was something eerie, supernatural, mysterious, and occult in these extremely powerful paintings. I was initially shocked. I did not quite understand what Pletka was driving at. Later, it dawned on me that Paul was not painting Indians at all, but was treating the transcendental essence of religion. I became intrigued. Philosophically, I have a certain fascination for some of the primitive religions. I began to see a 'taking apart' of what we consider sophisticated, contemporary religion, which is in reality based on magic—and the same logic applied thousands of years back."

Jerry Ravenscroft became beguiled by Pletka's work while the artist was enrolled at Colorado State University. Several years ago, Ravenscroft unearthed Weston La Barre's *The Ghost Dance* (Dell Publishing Co., Inc., New York, 1970), a book that probes the origins of religion. In it, he found clues helpful in the interpretation of Pletka's work. Ravenscroft contends, "Pletka is a painter of sacred culture. There is a difference between religion and magic, a basically psychological difference. Religion is an appeal to a single entity. Supernatural beliefs, on the other hand, bestow everything with power; you obtain that object's power by wearing it or eating it—which we know as communion—or in some way possessing it. What Pletka does with his paintings of Indians is portray sacred cultures and the way in which power sources so strongly influenced the people. He overwhelms his audience with it.

"A very common comment heard about Pletka's work is, 'It's amazing, but too powerful for me to live with.' I don't think very many people understand his work, but they feel it. I don't think even Pletka really understands how he's doing it. He is so involved that he literally becomes hypnotized by the artifact he's painting, just as the Indian was entranced a hundred years ago."

Though Pletka immerses himself in the sacred macrocosm of his subjects, he does not personally embrace their doctrine, in fact, he clings to no recognized system of religious belief. He emphasizes, "My religion is my painting."

While the post-Gothic movement influenced Pletka's philosophical and emotional approach to painting, he credits more recent artists with guiding his technical direction and style. Spanish painter and printmaker Francisco José de Goya (1746–1828) gave Pletka ideas about the drama of size with his monumental *Second of May* and *Third of May,* articulate commemorations of Spanish resistance to French invaders. Pletka has also been moved by the self-taught French surrealist Yves Tanguy (1900–1957) and German graphic artist Käthe Kollwitz (1867–1945), a staunch pacifist whose portrayals of the subjugated masses vibrate with anguish, and by the sensitivities of English painter Francis Bacon (b. 1910), a controversial artist known for his disturbing portraits of screaming figures trapped within obscure black cages.

Pletka reveres and shares an identity with others, including a number of twentieth-century artists: Grant Wood, painter of the famous satirical *Daughters of the American Revolution;* realist Paul Cadmus; painter Alton Pickens; Russian-born Peter Blume, who stirred a political cauldron with *The Eternal City,* a denunciation of Italian Fascism; abstract expressionists Franz Kline and Larry Rivers; and Ivan Le Lorraine Albright, the master of theatrical illumination and restless motion. Most particularly, Pletka identifies with Albright's *The Picture of Dorian Gray,* in which the wealth of detail and intimate revelation creates a bewildering maze that shocks the eye and wrenches the perspective.

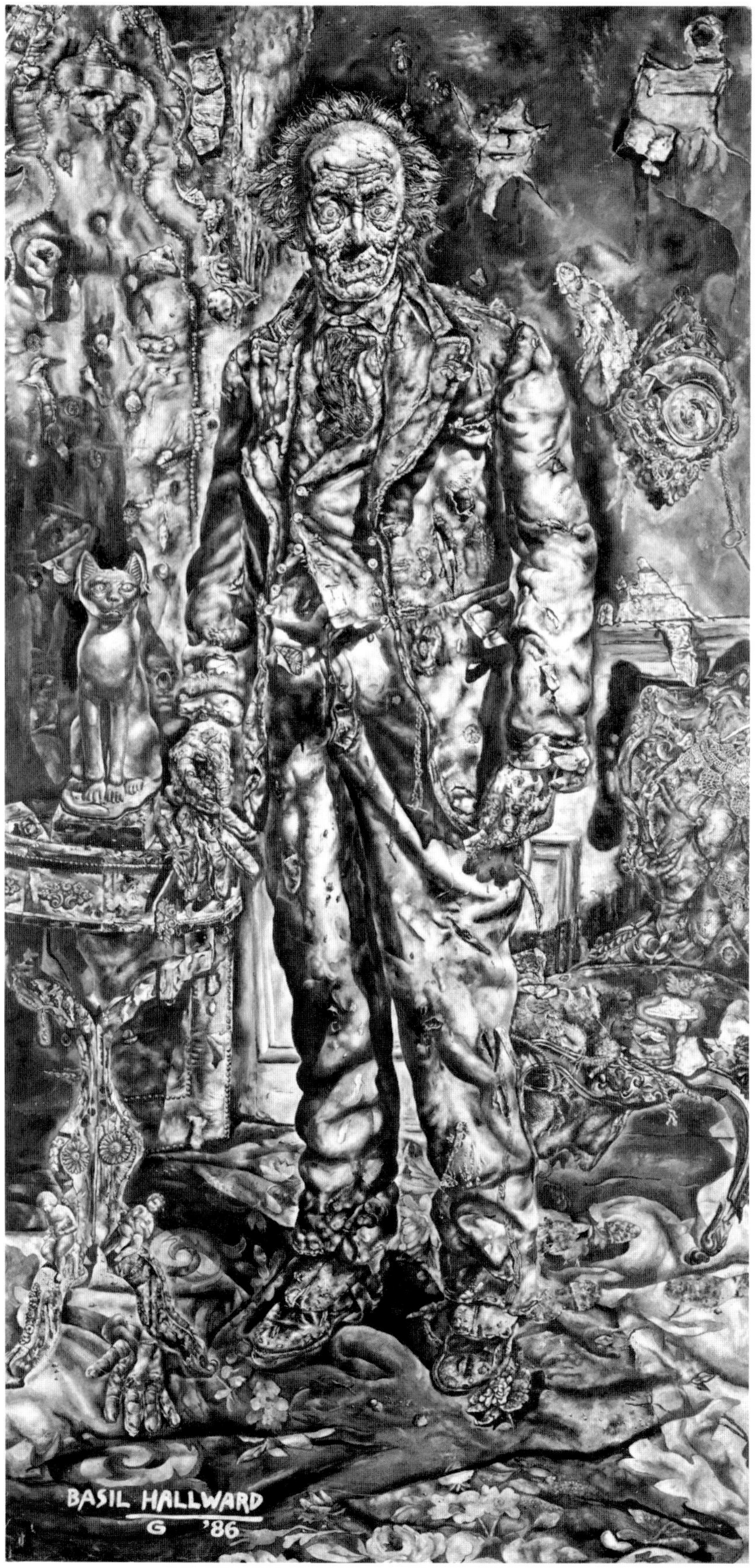

The Picture of Dorian Gray, by Ivan Le Lorraine Albright, 1943–44, oil on canvas, 85½″ x 42″, Collection of The Art Institute of Chicago. Albright painted this picture for the Metro Goldwyn Mayer movie based on Oscar Wilde's *Picture of Dorian Gray,* and inscribed it with the name of Basil Hallward, the person to whom the painting was attributed in the film.

Motives and Motifs

Artistic growth is, more than it is anything else, a refining of the sense of truthfulness. The stupid believe that to be truthful is easy; only the artist, the great artist, knows how difficult it is.

WILLA CATHER

Where is Paul Pletka going in his zealous crusade? What are these august Indians, sacrosanct birds, and portentous skulls trying to convey? Pletka denies his paintings are fueled by political acrimony or sentimentality. Yet, they are much more than historical illustrations. Though steeped in mysticism, they certainly are not an expression of traditional religious forms.

What, then, is their *raison d'être?*

"My function is to raise questions, not supply answers," Pletka stresses. "I must constantly probe. Every painting asks questions. I have never said I have any answers. I don't. I don't expect anyone to learn some specific lesson from a particular painting. But, if I can make that person wonder or reflect, fine. That's enough.

"There's a lot to be learned from the experiences of the past; vicissitudes and struggle have always been elements of civilization. At issue is how they are addressed and whether we learn anything from past failures and weaknesses. Maybe my paintings will serve as reminders. Whether applied to Indians or Penitentes or Egyptians, I'm concerned with man—his day-to-day relationship with his god, his fellow man, and nature. My paintings don't have much to do with political problems or social reform, per se. The main thrust is magic: ceremonialism, totemism, animism, and supernaturalism—occult drives suppressed in all of us. They were bared briefly in the Middle Ages, then cloaked behind a veil of dignity, if you will. I believe they are beginning to surface again. That's what these paintings are about, not Indian reservations or broken treaties or bloody battlefields. Additionally, I'm concerned with accomplishing great technical paintings. If that happens, I'm content. I'm not attempting, nor am I bright enough, to solve the world's problems, past or present."

While Pletka pointedly avoids lecturing through his paintings, his own appetite for knowledge is insatiable. A significant feature of his home is a collection of ethnological treasures and relics, representative of Nancy's and Paul's interest in art as a

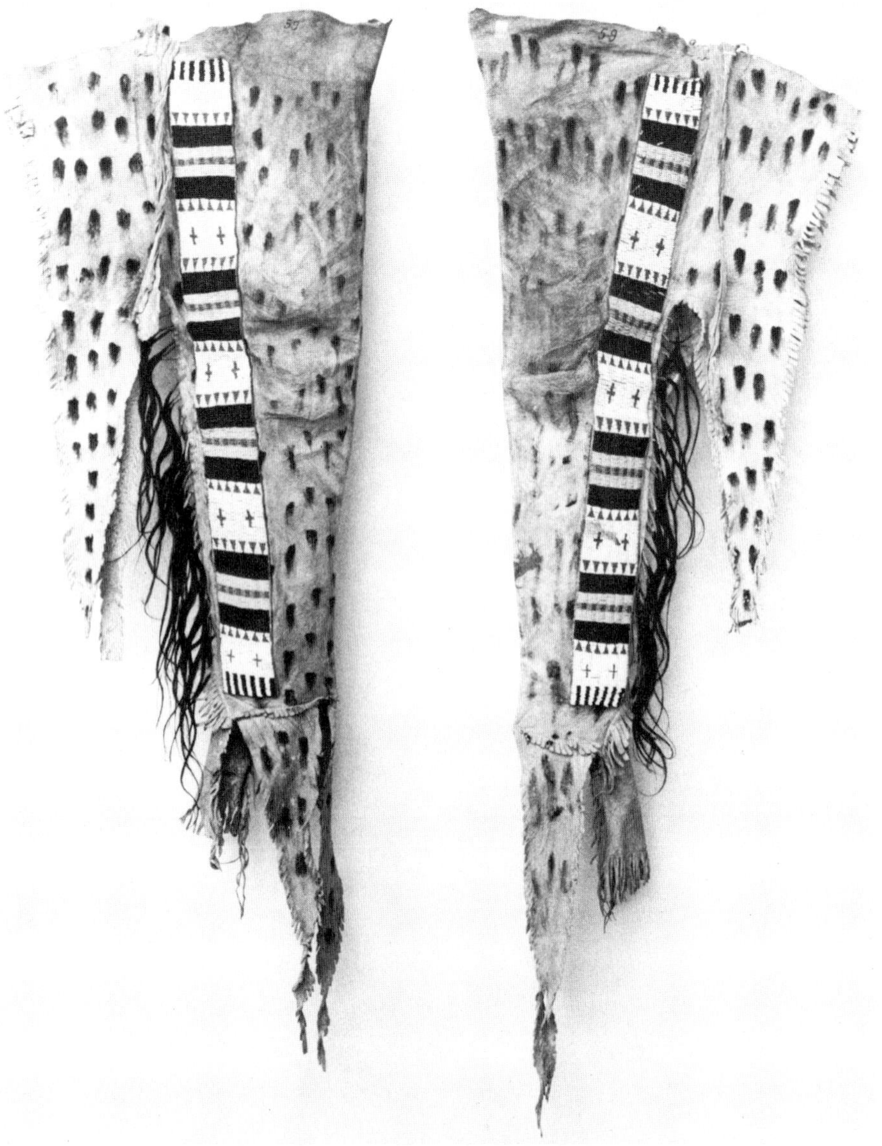

Left:
Pitahauerat Pawnee, ca. 1870. Native tanned buffalo hide, ochre and black paint, multi-colored glass beads, human hair. These leggings, although of slightly later origin and representative of a different tribe, provided the genesis for the leggings on "the departed one" in *Wakan Dagre*.

Below:
Eastern Sioux, ca. 1860. Wood, green and red paint, brass tacks. Reminiscent of specimens collected about 1833 in Minnesota, this carved flute with its blocky head and exaggerated beak looks like a wading bird. The talisman wedged under the arms of the bound human fetish in *The Bonds of Antiquity* is a replication of this artifact, and serves as a counterpart to the real heron also tied to the fetish.

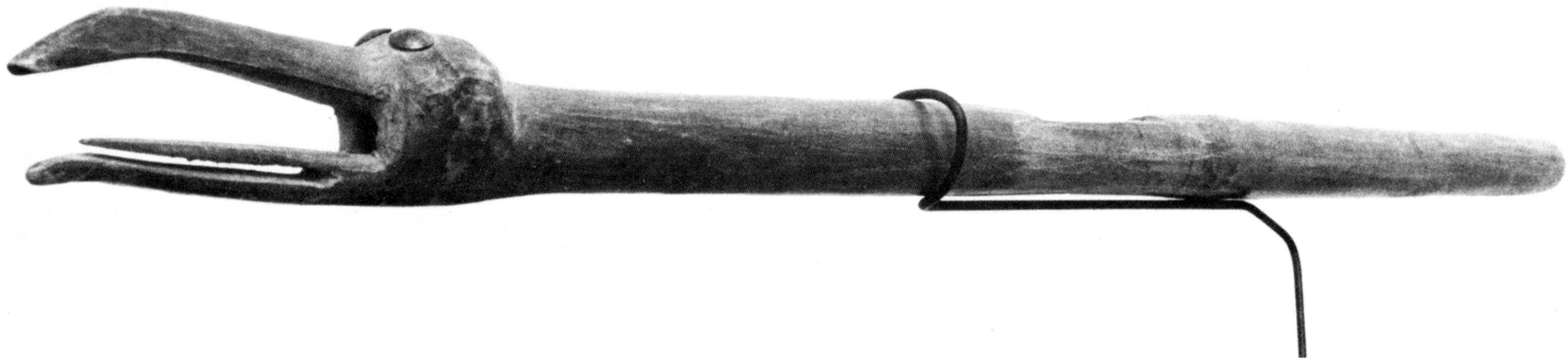

functional component of historical and ancient cultures. But, more than that, each item has served as a nexus to Pletka's proclivity for research; for his desire to know all that there is to know about the genesis, accretion, use, design, and meaning of appurtenances that have, over time, shaped this global village.

He is committed to accuracy, and only to satisfy the uncompromising demands of composition will he insert a superfluous bird or modify the dimensions of a shield or vary the color of a blanket. "But," he notes, "I would never put a Java sparrow in the middle of the Plains." A feverish reader, Pletka devours data and has a retention rate that astounds his friends and associates. Because so much material has been recorded about the Reservation Indian period of the late nineteenth century, he feels a duty to utilize those records and faithfully reflect history. He pores over battle accounts, annals of the pioneer migration, descriptions of complex religious rites, reports of costumes and body ornaments, archaeological and anthropological treatises. He studies in detail the specifications of beadwork, medicine bundles, drums, and sacred war clubs. He indefatigably pursues any tangible or spiritual element of Indian culture and lore.

"When I was a youngster, and first enchanted with costume, lore, and artifacts, I would sometimes pretend I was an Indian. I soon realized that was not intellectually reasonable. I am not an Indian. I am simply an interpreter."

Pletka is quick to remind one that the differences between cultures are far less significant than the similarities. The Plains Indians of the 1880s may have existed in a spiritual and physical world both curious and inconceivable by modern standards, but they were nonetheless people laboring to adapt their human nature to the demands of their surroundings. The myth of strangeness or alien difference is one Pletka hopes to dispel.

He did not deductively select Indians as subjects; he has felt an intuitive affinity to their culture for as long as he can remember. "I was literally captivated by Indian attitudes, medicines, and witchcraft," he says. "The subject had not been satisfactorily approached through art, and I wanted to explore that facet of human history."

As fate would have it, his initial artistic efforts were imperfectly timed. Although Indian arts and crafts enjoyed high repute in the early 1970s, paintings containing a western flavor were automatically dismissed as gimmicky. Pletka was faced with the Sisyphian task of breaking through an iron cliché to find serious acceptance.

"I had a tough time," he says, "dealing with the inevitability of painting Indians and the stigma that labeled such work as only pretty, mindless, and decorative. The internal struggle was terrible, because I really did want to be accepted—but on my own terms. I wanted to break ground with a new approach; I wanted to make a fresh statement about a subject sorely in need of exposure and decent, serious treatment. It was akin to fighting an uphill battle."

But fight he did.

During this period he received the additional advice that Indian art must be created by Indian artists, not charading Anglos scheming to cash in on the treasures of Native American heritage. Such opinions infuriated Pletka. He fumed silently and painted his Indians: not John Ford Indians, not George Catlin Indians, not drugstore Indians, but Paul Pletka Indians.

In his earliest efforts, he found himself typecasting Indians as resourceless prey of the white frontier. He says, "Originally, I wanted to show the down side of Indians, to show how they had been brutalized by the system. I painted them as victims, people who had been thrust into the twentieth century without a survival kit, rendered almost invisible by an unfortunate set of circumstances." In Pletka's early paintings of turn-of-the-century Indians, the figures are fat, slightly grotesque, and isolated, wearing ragtag outfits. The faces are fragmented and torn as though they are actually masks, representing what Pletka describes as a statement he needed to make. He soon modified that phase, and stopped treating Indians as fractured victims. He gave them more dignity.

As a collector, Pletka is seduced by the Indians' material culture. As a researcher, he is absorbed by their past. As a colorist, he is enchanted by the kaleidoscopic array of costumes and trappings. As a painter interested in liturgical themes, he is intoxicated by the scope and malleability of Indian magic. He seems to recognize an opportunity to wield that potent polytheism as a mirror of man's soul and feels that Indians are the ideal vehicle.

Pletka has come to the conclusion that Indian religion is a way of life, unlike organized religions that exist separately from the secular world. He finds no secular arena in Indian life and views the Plains Indians as a microcosm of pure, unfettered people, a reflection of the human experience. Plains Indians speak to him more so than South Seas tribes or most African groups. He does very little exploration of the Pueblo Indians because their tightly prescribed iconography leaves little room for creative extrapolation. Northwest Coast tribes execute beautiful sculpture, but offer scant opportunity for interpretative latitude.

"The Plains people don't have those heavy religious constraints. That's what I find so wonderful about their religion. It changes at will, fitting whatever situation comes up. The military societies were loose organizations with tremendous versatility. A man could have a dream, have it interpreted by the elders, and then fashion clothing or readjust his lifestyle according to the dream's meaning. This kind of latitude allows for innumerable combinations in paintings.

"The period I'm primarily interested in has to do with the nomadic warrior society. For the most part, I'm treating the horse culture, which was operative for about one hundred years, from the late 1700s to the late 1800s. The pure Plains culture was dying by 1850, and by 1880 was basically gone. I tend to focus on those nomadic tribes, because they were steeped in magic, less structured, and very colorful." He adds wryly, "What's more, they used lots of feathers, one of my favorite devices."

By 1900, most of the traditional customs of the Plains tribes had been diluted by the westward population surge. Fences entangled the countryside. Indians were herded onto reservations, and their firm marriage with nature began to dissolve. Robbed of liberty, they watched with helpless bewilderment as hordes of white men swarmed over their once-fertile land. Not surprisingly, the Plains Indians' ties to magic frayed. The power of mysticism evaporated, closing the doors on a provocative doctrine in which man pursued nature's strengths while respecting her fragility. Pletka's paintings do not explore far beyond these times of political and social upheavals.

"Mechanized America killed the magic and the mystery," Pletka laments. "I can't think of a better way to express it. It was cut off at the knees. The Indians lost their identity, and there was no chance to regroup. The reservations demoralized them. Indians who were sent to Washington, D.C., couldn't believe the numbers of white men they saw. They returned to their tribes with stories of uncountable white populations.

"The warrior societies collapsed. The medicine failed. Even the birds failed them. Kingfishers, for example, were powerful bullet-proofing agents; such protective measures were a very serious matter with the Plains Indians. An individual's success in battle might well depend on whether his personal medicine was working that day. That's where the latitude of their religion steps in. It's like having a bad dream but being able to manipulate some of the events while you're still asleep. The Indians had rationalizations to explain their way out of tight spots: if Red Bird's medicine didn't work one day, then there must be some logical reason. He did something wrong. He didn't follow the dream properly, and thus lost his power. The advance of civilization soon engulfed that kind of reasoning, ruining both their material culture and their religious purpose."

Through the course of events, Indians became refugees, living in poverty on government-designated reservations. It was not a savory moment in our history, but one from which Pletka believes we can learn a great deal. He hopes to add to the awareness and understanding of the events and injustices of that experience.

The Pletka purview, however, is not limited to the Plains Indians. The shy and peaceful Tarahumara Indians of the Sierra Madre Occidental in northern Mexico are the focus of a 1981 painting, *Tarahumara.* Pletka's interest in this isolated culture, numbering no more than 40,000, was stimulated by their intriguing ritualization of native rites in combination with Catholicism.

The Pueblo Indians are evident in Pletka's 1976 acrylic, *Hawikuh,* a portrayal of the Zuñi olla carriers. The two women serve as pedestals for early examples of Zuñi pottery, a reminder of the artist's consuming interest in cultural paraphernalia.

Another major subject departure occurred when Pletka moved to Tesuque in 1977. He began to study the history and rituals of Los Hermanos Penitentes, a flagellant religious organization that flourished in New Mexico and southern Colorado during the 1800s and remains active in scattered hamlets of the Sangre de Cristo mountains north of Santa Fe. This Hispanic lay society has its roots in the ceremonial aspects of the Roman Catholic Church. The group's spirit of penance erupts most fervently during Holy Week, when members of the brotherhood severely scourge themselves, conduct a mock crucifixion, and melodramatically re-enact events leading to the Resurrection. Some public processions occur, but most Penitente activities take place secretly behind the doors of *moradas,* brotherhood meeting houses. Published accounts of Penitente rites are scarce and sketchy and raise more questions than they answer. Pletka absorbed all of the written material he could locate on the subject, then turned to another source for information, a friend and longtime admirer of the artist's work, Larry Frank.

Frank lives in an Hispanic village north of Taos. An authority on historic Pueblo pottery and New Mexican *santos,* he has studied and observed the Penitente lifestyle for two decades. He says, "We bought a *morada* and five acres, sight unseen, for $1,750. We were the first Anglos in Arroyo Hondo, and community acceptance was not immediate. We've never witnessed the really secret aspects of Penitente rituals; as an Anglo, you can only go so far. I've been inside Penitente *moradas* and seen all the equipment, and we attended the *Tinieblas,* which recreates the chaotic period of the three days immediately following the Crucifixion when the world was in darkness and turmoil without the guidance of Christ. The people enter the *morada* with all their equipment, and they kneel and pray, seeking blessings for their animals. Certain *santos* are blindfolded, and candles representing the twelve disciples are extinguished one by one until it's totally dark.

"Then all hell breaks loose. The *matracas,* noisemakers, are twirling around and around. High-pitched wooden flutes, *pitas,* sound eerily. Big sticks bang around, and huge chains with enormous links are rattled and swung through the air. The cacophony is ungodly. It's very theatrical."

While still prevalent in tiny Hispanic retreats, the Penitente groups, or Brothers of Blood, are all but invisible, the result of years of harassment by gawking tourists and stern ultimatums from Roman Catholic Church leaders, who long ago forbade self-flagellation and simulated crucifixions. Frank explains, "The Penitentes took it upon themselves to relieve the weight of sin from everyone's shoulders. One way was to re-enact as literally as possible the ordeal Christ underwent. In their view, it is hypocritical to go to church on Sunday, say a token prayer, and undo it the next day. That's considered cheap, easy, and fashionable. The Penitentes prefer, instead, to be reminded of Christ's actual suffering."

After more than two years of absorbing information and formulating mental paintings, Pletka decided to tackle the Penitente theme. Again, he believed that the topic, although dealing with a sacred quirk, had universal applications. What the Penitentes performed so literally, man through the ages had practiced internally: self-inflicted psychological torture to assuage guilt and guarantee salvation. Pletka says, "As far as the specific ceremonial aspects go, flagellation is common. You can find self-flagellant societies on every continent. One reason I got interested in the Penitentes was the Sun Dance, a basic religious act among Plains Indians of the nineteenth century. The Sun Dance was a renewal ceremony whereby the participants sometimes gave pieces of flesh or otherwise inflicted self-torture. The body was the only thing a man could rightfully own, because it was believed the spirits owned everything else. So the ultimate gift to the One Above was your own flesh and blood. Sitting Bull sacrificed one hundred pieces of flesh during a Sun Dance. He had his cousin punch the awl into his arm and snip off the flesh with scissors. That same attitude is behind Penitente rituals, giving all you can of yourself, cleansing yourself."

Pletka's artistic trek into Penitente territory spawned the *Las Muertas* triptych, fraught with death symbols and stark cadaverous images found not only macabre but repellent by some.

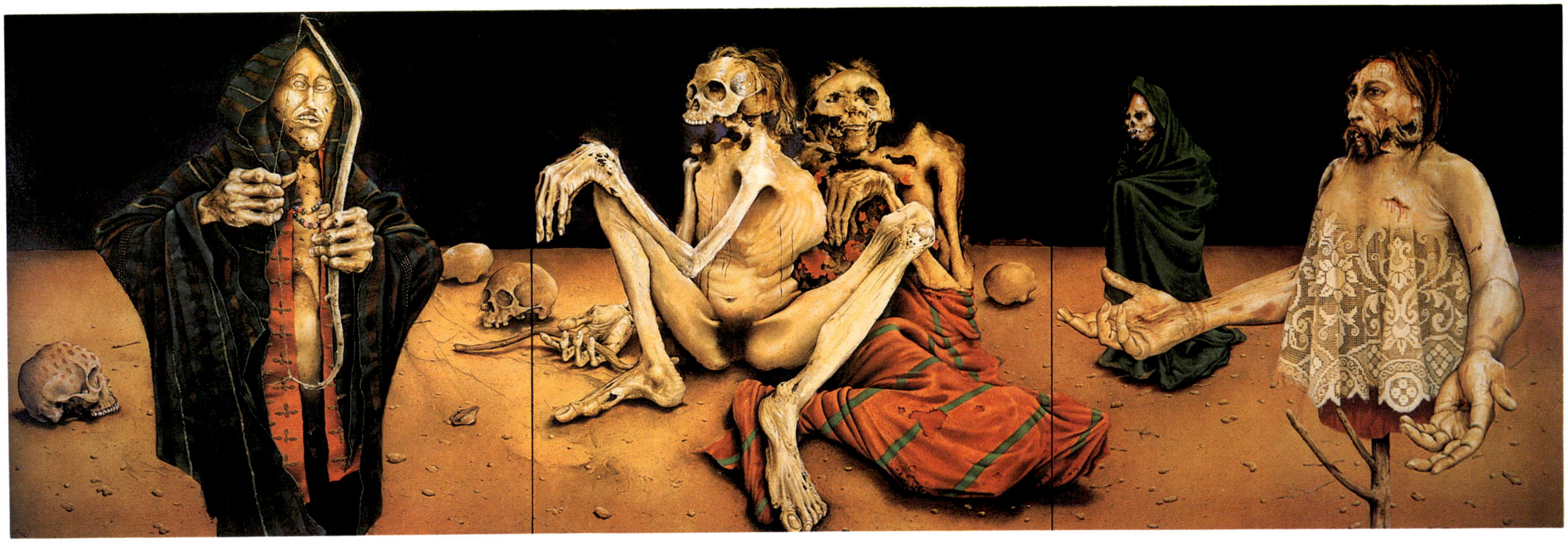

Las Muertas, 1980, acrylic on linen canvas, triptych, 48 x 144

No doubt Pletka's most controversial painting, *Las Muertas* depicts many of the beliefs and ceremonies of the Penitentes; however, a southwestern Indian flavor is suggested in the skull with the red spots and the mummy behind the seated female. The painting is replete with powerful and cryptic symbols of Christianity and death.

Larry Frank says of Pletka's expedition into Penitente themes: "I think it is a marvelous move that invokes an entirely new ambience. It encompasses a spirit light years from his Indian series. He is dealing with death here. There is a judgment, an implicit morality, a reminder of man's brief time on earth. The Indian is more removed and romantic, because frankly, no one understands the Indian world. It's as alienated as New Guinea or another planet. But when you talk about the Christian tradition and modern religion, it hits all of us. It stares us in the face. Brightly colored Indians, particularly historical ones, have nothing to do with us. How can we connect with the Sioux in 1838? The Penitente message is a little more harrowing. It's nearer. It breathes on us."

Most modern western societies shun contemplation of death, viewing it as an inevitable, but negative occurrence. At odds with this are those cultures that see death as a way to another life, which may be entirely better. Pletka asserts that curiosity about death is natural, that it should not be suppressed, and that what the Indians and Penitentes feel is at least honest. "We are trapped by the veneer of our civilization. Important feelings are sublimated to a series of learned mannerisms. I think that's why my pictures touch people at a visceral level; they penetrate the veneer and hit them where they live."

Le Tour De Force

The artists must be sacrificed to their art. Like the bees, they must put their lives into the sting they give.

RALPH WALDO EMERSON

The finished painting is an iridescent arrangement of slate, ocher, turquoise, madder, apricot, and maroon. Ironically, its genesis is often one of the motionless images of Pletka's monochromatic dreams. When he awakes, the stark fragments still vivid in his memory are transcribed into sketches and notebooks. They then undergo a metamorphosis that may stretch three or four years. Nurtured in Pletka's head, they mature gradually. A swatch of color here, a filament of detail there. Finally, they emerge from a mental cocoon onto a colossal canvas, where they are expected to thrive. "I'll mull ideas in the back of my mind for long periods," Pletka says. "I thought about *New Mexico Landscape* for two years before approaching the canvas. I rarely do anything on the spur of the moment. The painting is usually a combination of instinct and research, a closely knit mixture that can't be divorced. The idea is refined until it's cogent."

In the process of committing figment to pigment, Pletka is not only his sharpest critic but a ruthless employer who drives himself to the brink of mental and physical exhaustion. The factory tyrants of Upton Sinclair's *The Jungle* pale next to Pletka's expectations for himself. The very paintings that earn the unabashed praise of browsers in the gallery are subjected to compulsive scrutiny in the studio, where the artist agonizes and ruminates over a brush stroke that may delineate a wisp of hair.

"When everything clicks, it's such a joy," Pletka beams, adding glumly, "It doesn't happen very often. Painting is very difficult for me. It's never easy. People assume it is because I put out a certain quality of work in a professional manner. It's not only a struggle between me and the canvas, a struggle of skills—it's a mental battle. The real gut-wrenching part is the first ten strokes. Is it spontaneous enough? Will it be fresh? Or hackneyed? Is it properly drawn? Have I achieved the posture I want, the tilt? Is it pretty? If it isn't sensitive, if it isn't poetic, I won't be able to salvage it at that point, and I'll scrap it. This all happens in the first half hour.

"Many times the canvas is either erased or thrown out. It's tough getting started, and it's tough working on a ten-foot canvas, where I've got three acres of beads to paint. Then it's hard to keep going, because I've already made the statement. But I know it's not finished correctly unless I give complete attention to every detail. It requires ultimate concentration."

Pletka freely admits to the very common trait of recoiling when criticized but is quick to add that he is not totally immune to suggestion. One of his cherished memories is when noted artist Robert Peak visited his studio. "I had been working on *Red Talkers* for eight months and it still hadn't clicked. The two figures in front doing the bison charge at each other were really bothering me. Peak took one look and understood immediately. 'It's simple,' he said, 'you've just been painting on it too long. You're trying to show depth by bringing the light up from behind. That's theoretically correct, except you ought to know better than that. Try filling in the space with dark paint, instead. You'll see—it'll turn out right!' He was absolutely correct. The figures rushed to the foreground."

In spite of the agony of perfection he describes, Pletka likes to paint. Over the years, however, he has learned to pace himself. He no longer risks his health with marathon sessions and is usually content with more traditional working hours.

"But on some days, I have to fight to get *anything* done, because I'd rather have my nose in a book. I don't go to town a lot, because I tend to hang around. I used to hit every Indian artifact shop and art gallery in Santa Fe. Now I stay home for long periods."

In preparing to paint, the first requirement is solitude, necessary to permit a tranquil state of mind. Temperamental and unpredictable, Pletka has been known to bash walls when disruptions shattered his fragile peace. "Anything can set me off," he says. "I'm very volatile. I lash out at things and get very depressed. I have absolute, total anger. Sometimes, it's released into my paintings in the form of flamboyance. Painting is my therapy. Without it, I'd be institutionalized. That's not a joke.

"When I work, I need solitude. I wrap myself in a cocoon of aloneness. I never allow anyone in the studio anymore. I don't really like even Nancy in there and won't allow her in when I'm starting a painting or doing something particularly difficult. I'm rude to people who come over, or I'm so spaced out and preoccupied I don't pay any attention to them. I know I've offended several people that way. That's one reason I live so far out in Tesuque. I picked someplace no one would find. I mean, if I could be another twenty miles out of town, I'd be there. It's not that I don't like people. I just can't concentrate when they're around.

"Nancy is very good about this. She knows when I can't be disturbed. We don't go anywhere. She takes care of every communication with the outside world, every nuance and subtlety that usually requires my attention. If I'm interrupted, it takes me a week to get square again. It throws me into a blue funk and I can't function."

The remoteness Tesuque affords has been a positive force for Pletka: "When I first started painting, I could work under any conditions. The barking dogs—no problem; the doorbell—no problem. Then, I had no privacy. Now, I need the isolation I have.

Tesuque is tranquilly alive, a beautiful, envigorating luxury."

Despite the time Pletka invests in painting, he is not prolific, completing only seven to ten paintings annually. He may spend up to six months on one. Because he has grown more meticulous and deliberate, he abandons fewer efforts midstream. A decade ago, his pace was hurried and his planning inexact. Half his paintings were rejected before completion. Today, only one in four is eliminated.

Once an image is firmly visualized, Pletka draws preliminary thumbnail sketches. Elements of the proposed painting sometimes are cut out and positioned on a dummy canvas, and choreographed into several versions until he is pleased with the composition. When the rehearsals end, Pletka draws the fundamental shapes and lines onto a canvas, which he primes and stretches himself. Though fanatical in his demand for historical, geographic, and anatomical accuracy, the artist rarely relies on photographs to chart his course. He explains, "Photographs can be deadly, because too much is done for you. If you can use them without leaning on them, fine. For instance, a photograph can serve as an excellent corrective aide when analyzing the proper bend of a wrist."

Faced with a stark canvas, Pletka feels exhilaration. Nancy says, "When he's starting a painting, it becomes his own private love affair. He won't let anybody see it. He feels there is a jinx period, when the painting must be protected from all eyes. After he's worked on it three or four days, he lets me see it. From then on, he's slightly distracted all the time. He works from 9:00 or 10:00 in the morning until dinner and sometimes an hour or two in the evening. It's impossible for him to go to sleep early. He plays solitaire over and over and over."

The preliminary drawing stage includes hours of frenetic activity. When there's a radio in the studio, Pletka blares rock music. Otherwise, he switches on the television and paces while awaiting inspiration. "I listen to the soap operas on TV, which are infinitely better than game shows," he says. "The soaps are just noise and noise helps. I do a lot of pacing and staring at the canvas. If I'm doing a good job, I'll pat myself on the back and wallow in the pleasure I feel. If I'm having difficulty, I'll lash out at myself and remind myself of what a really rotten painter I am."

When Pletka feels detached or overwhelmed by dimensions, he will focus on a small portion of a figure, flesh it out with contour, shading, and detail, and thereby set the tone for the entire field. The drawing must straddle the fence between a rough sketch and a precise blueprint of detail. Next, tubes of acrylic paint are stacked within reach. He squeezes blobs of color onto his palette, a two-by-eight balanced on a sawhorse. His jeans become an alternate palette. (Pletka once gave an especially paint-mottled pair of pants to Santa Fe gallery owner Forrest Fenn, who unabashedly labeled and displayed them with the noteworthy palettes of Gaspard and Fechin, among others.) Initially, pigment is applied thinly to create a color scheme. If he has misread the hue pattern, the acrylic film facilitates quick and easy adjustments. He carefully calculates how the color will enhance the painting's rhythm, then moves on to the background. Later, figures are blocked in and refined layer by layer, as color and line are incorporated to lend movement to the mass. Finally, detail.

"That's when I start to wear out," Pletka says.

"That's when the patience comes in. After three months of working on one canvas that's so large it almost engulfs you, you can't see anything else. I want to explode. My peripheral vision is fairly good, but when I can see only canvas on both sides of me, I have to grit my teeth to keep going. If I find something wrong at one end of the painting, I panic, because I think I'll have to change something at the other end too, which will mean altering this or that figure; pretty soon I'm unglued. It once put me in the hospital with heart palpitations and hyperventilation.

"After every painting, it's true, I spend a few days in bed, because I have no physical strength left. *Wakan Dagre,* the four-figure painting I keep in the living room, was a solid effort of six months, day after day. During the last month of work, I wanted to lose my concentration. I was wishing I had an apprentice to apply those yards of beads. But I could never do that. My work is too personal. I finished the painting and then spent two weeks in bed. That's why I'm keeping it."

Pletka is hesitant to place a label on his style of painting, though he concedes he is in a neo-surrealist phase that demands color intensity and conscientious regard for detail. He says, "Right now, my pictures are tight, static, brittle. When I exhaust this phase, I'll loosen up again, I suppose. I milk an idea or technique for all it's worth and then virtually abandon it. I'll keep what I think will be applicable on the next plateau. There are things I don't know yet, things I've never heard of, things that have never been done that I ought to be developing, or attempting to develop. The skills are there. After all, I've been practicing since I was four years old."

Pletka's compositions have undergone a legion of transformations since then. Many transitions, such as the move to larger canvases, were gradual. His works did not reach gargantuan proportions on a steady basis until 1973, with the birth of *Roman Nose in Death.* Pletka notes, *"Roman Nose in Death* was a breakthrough for me. I had been moving toward the idea of monumental works, but there was a prejudice in the market. People simply didn't do large paintings of Indians or western subjects, an irony considering the West is by its very nature larger than life. You were supposed to do nice little pictures to hang over sofas. *Roman Nose in Death* was painted on my patio in Grand Junction. It was unmanageable in the house. Every day, it was a matter of jockeying it outside. And then, 'Oh, God, it's raining,' and I'd grab it and race back into the house."

One Pletka hallmark involves displaying figures in a progressive sweep that carries the eye horizontally across the canvas, a device used especially in his bird groupings. More often, Pletka's figures take on mountainous shapes; the head forms the apex and the torso, with its thick garments, widens to a weighty base that anchors the image and gives it strength. These pyramidal shapes are reminiscent of the geological formations Pletka so admires in the Utah landscape.

In the late 1970s, another change occurred. Pletka began straying from his trademark backdrops of grainy, dripping washes that produced a stunning luster and a remarkable texture. He started to view his subjects through a wide-angle lens, resulting in greater depth and breadth. Backgrounds of stark desert vistas under skies with restless, hulking clouds replaced scabrous curtains of muted color.

Pletka's palette has remained relatively stable,

though he tends toward periods of preference for certain shades. His color sense is emphatically eastern European: brilliant, almost garish, splotches of primary colors against flat grays and black. "I'm abysmally stuck on red," he says. "I'm destined to use red in everything, a lucky coincidence, since red is the sacred Indian color, the color of blood. I don't know why it appeals to me so much. I like warm colors. I prefer using warm colors and grays and black and then counterpointing them with sharp stabs of cool. Recently, I've discovered green. The longer I paint, the more pure my colors become. I guess I'll reach a summit and turn back again, but right now I'm favoring very bright colors."

The characters in Pletka's pieces, whether they be Paiute, Pawnee, Ponca, or even Penitente, share an uncanny resemblance while maintaining singular and intriguing identities. "I have a set perception of what Indians and Hispanics look like," Pletka says. "I vary each figure's looks by empathizing with the person. I ask myself what kind of personality would fit this situation. Then I proceed to inject the face and body and posture into the figure. Each one varies, but when I try to stray too far, my eye will correct me. It will override my brain and reel me in."

Among the logotypes of Pletka's work is the recurring appearance of unusually large and dramatically stationed hands. In *Crow Indian,* for example, the figure's right hand seems poised to snatch the passerby. The same effect is achieved with *Takes Back Twice.* Hands also are employed to inject motion into a composition or to steer the viewer through a curve, as in *Oh Holy Raven* and *Kills Night.* A sense of stoicism is attained through the extended arm of *Cacique,* while the elegant hands of *Elk Song* exude a pulsating rhythm. In many portraits, including *Skin Walker* and particularly *Leroy,* folded hands underscore a fierce dignity. Clearly, hands function as integral components of each painting's physical and emotional strategy.

"The largeness of the hands came about as part of triangular distortion," Pletka says. "When you look up from the base of the triangle, your perception changes. I started doing that unconsciously until the hands became larger and larger, almost reaching a preposterous size. One day I started studying them and decided they were too damn large. I reduced them, consciously. That was four or five years ago. Now they're down to a more realistic size again. The large hands are an important visual device. But, the truth is they began as the result of a bad drawing habit. I know that's not the answer everyone wants to hear. People want to believe the hands are large because the Indians work with their hands and are close to nature. An anthropologist once asked me, 'Why do your Indians have such large hands? All my Indian friends want to know, because they in fact admire small hands and feet.' You can see I'm not trying to second-guess Indians."

Birds play another important role in Pletka's paintings, just as feathers are a constant ingredient that add grace and flourish. Whether used as a solitary embellishment, as in *Nota 'A* and *The Horse Thief,* or festooned in dramatic cascades, as in *Sings to the Wind* and *Star Lookers,* feathers provide a means of breaking away from bulk while garnishing often harsh stances with a dainty filigree. Birds in Pletka's works range from the dismembered whooping crane in *Takes Back Twice* to tiny bound fetishes in *Strawberries for Tobacco* to symbolic extensions of the fig-

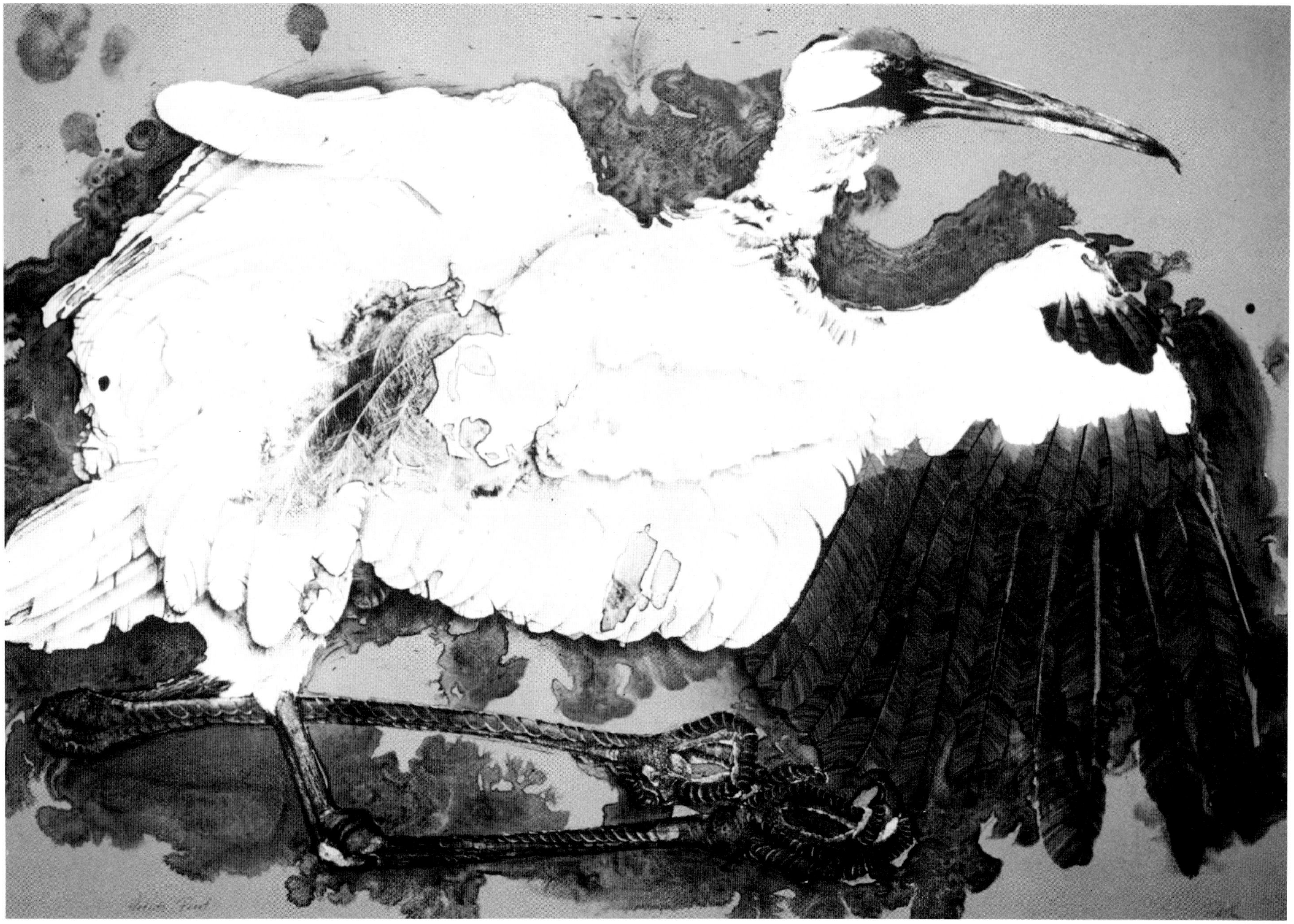

Grus Americana, 1977, color lithograph, 30 x 44

ure's flesh and soul in *Hail Eagle*. Occasionally, the birds thrust themselves into the central focus, overpowering even the most austere and magnetic figures, as is evident in *Bacu Sua* and *Oldest Whose Ears Hang Backward*. Frequently, birds perform simply as beautiful ornaments completing a harmonious composition, as in *Cacique*.

"My father always liked birds," Pletka muses. "He liked animals in general and was an amateur taxidermist. Our family visited the San Diego Zoo a lot, and the bird section was fabulous. I would pick up stray feathers and use them to make costumes. There's no explaining it, but I'm drawn to birds. I feel a closeness, and they satisfy an aesthetic sense in me. Besides all of which, birds are important in Indian religion. For instance, the eagle was thought to be a messenger to the sun, because he flew higher than the rest.

"Technically, birds work in my paintings because they have a nice weight to them. They provide an interesting contradiction; first there's a pleasant visual weight then whoosh, they fly away. Feathers also attract me. I have a natural proclivity toward line and have to consciously fight to work mass into my pictures. My eye sees things in lines—must be bad coloring-book training. Feathers are merely a pattern of lines, of ribs. That appeals to me."

Symbols are common in Pletka's paintings, especially religious and death emblems, giving further testimony to his post-Gothic tendencies. He employs the cross for both its immaculate design and wide interpretations. In Penitente representations, the cross functions as a traditional Christian icon. But in Indian iconography, it adopts multiple meanings, from a delineation of the four directions to an embodiment of the dragonfly, considered a bullet-proofing power.

Skulls and skeletons entertain Pletka. "Bones are wonderful. For years, I didn't feel I had the maturity or technical ability to tackle them. I waited. In the first tests, some were unsuccessful, and I scrapped those. I took up physiology just to learn to draw them. They are sculpture, and they challenge me. The lines and shapes of the skull are particularly fascinating."

Despite many common denominators, no Pletka imitates another Pletka. Each painting projects a temperament, complexion, and charm of its own, without a shopworn thread or mechanical stitch in its fabric. Consequently, Pletka deals with them as warm friends, and it disheartens him to say goodbye. He says, "I know it's not professional, but I miss them."

Consanquinity

Only through art can we get outside of ourselves and know another's view of the universe which is not the same as ours and see landscapes which would otherwise have remained unknown to us like the landscapes of the moon.

MARCEL PROUST

Pletka tells the tale of connections—the ancestry and relationships of people, customs, beliefs, attitudes, behaviors, fears, and desires. He expresses the relativity of the time warp that intervenes or circumscribes perception of these experiences.

Strangely, he has little concern with whether his message is received or with how it is translated by others. His art is his own personal experience—it is in its process of creation, and ultimate culmination, that Pletka revels.

When he began work on *Las Muertas,* the harrowing triptych that remains his most controversial painting, he was warned that there was no audience for such a theme. "I prepared for *Las Muertas* for three years," he says. "I was tremendously fascinated by the Penitente concept; this was an idea whose time had come. I finally got enough nerve to tackle it, and said to myself, 'I'm going to paint exactly what I want to paint and I don't give a damn if it sells or sees the light of day.' Technically, *Las Muertas* is one of my best pieces. Predictably, the subject matter—especially the graphic female skeletal form with obvious religious and sexual connotations—has been totally misunderstood by some people."

The creative process of *Slippery Eye,* his best portrait to date, personifies the intellectual persuasion of the artist. He was first intrigued by a particular work of Karl Bodmer, *A Bison Painted Robe,* discovered by Pletka during one of his relentless pursuits of knowledge.

Bodmer had been employed by Prince Maximilian of Weid to accompany him on an expedition to America's northwestern plain in 1833. Maximilian's party spent that winter in the Upper Missouri region at Fort Clark near one of the principal Mandan villages. Bodmer's assignment was to document the expedition. Unlike many early artists on the plains, Bodmer, a native of Switzerland, had received formal training; his reputation for fidelity was unsurpassed. It was during the stay at Fort Clark that Mato-tope, second chief and hero of the Mandan nation, presented Maximilian with a robe. Now housed

The InterNorth Art Foundation, Joslyn Art Museum, Omaha, Nebraska

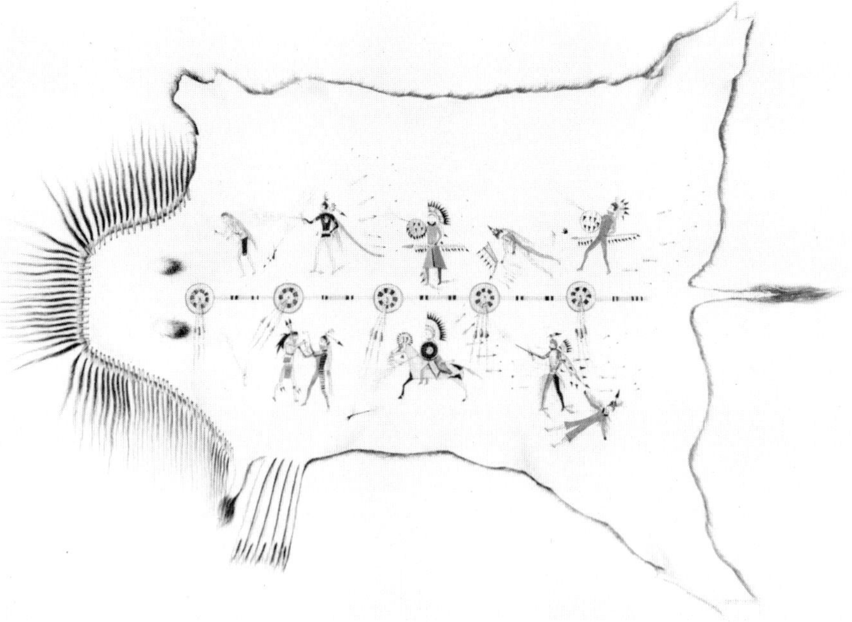

A Bison Painted Robe by Karl Bodmer, depicting Mato-Tope's hand-to-hand combat with a Cheyenne chief.

in the Stuttgart Museum, Stuttgart, Germany, the bison robe had been decorated by Mato-tope with pictures of his war exploits. It became the subject of one of Bodmer's most famous paintings.

Convinced of the authenticity of Bodmer's rendition, Pletka became immersed in a study of the robe. He was particularly intrigued by a small figure in the lower right hand corner, wearing striped leggings, a swallow-tail military coat, and a hair-fringed shirt. The more he studied, the more certain he became that the figure to which he was drawn, this Indian of the northern plains, was probably a Cree. A catalytic process had begun—his intellectual interest had stimulated a creative longing that became *Slippery Eye,* in whose bearing and brooding is seen the age-old contemplation of the imponderables of existence.

A pinnacle of Pletka's personal consanguinity is *The Bonds of Antiquity,* finished in the summer of 1982. This provocative painting stands in summation, consummating the use of symbols and talismans so significant to Pletka's earlier works. The figures are bound and decorated just like the fetishes appended to them. The stark reality of this painting is that the characters are becoming victims of their own beliefs. Dogma that may have at one time preserved their sacred beliefs now holds them captive, restraining their forward progression. Blinded by the pervasive blanket of tribalism, they stand rooted in place, bound by the very beliefs and attitudes that once saved them from extinction.

If, in *The Bonds of Antiquity,* he has summarized, has he concluded his explorations of the chasms that separate and similarities that bind? Or, has he once again invited closure on one chapter that he may begin another?

Commentary might well be found in Pletka's study of the Crucifixion. This immense, unfinished canvas stood across the studio as a sentinel during the artistic progression of *The Bonds of Antiquity.* He had started work on it earlier, but put it aside when inspired by an exploration of self-inflicted bondage. Later, refreshed, he once again focused his attention on this stimulating, yet enervating, contemplation of the Trinity.

"In order to better understand the workings of the body under the stress of such a situation, I constructed a cross and had Nancy tie me to it," he says. "What I had suspected was true. The back, unlike its portrayal in some early European paintings, tends to hyper-extend into a severe arch."

A close look at the partly finished canvas shows Christ flanked by two thieves, superimposed on a

Cradoc-Bagshaw

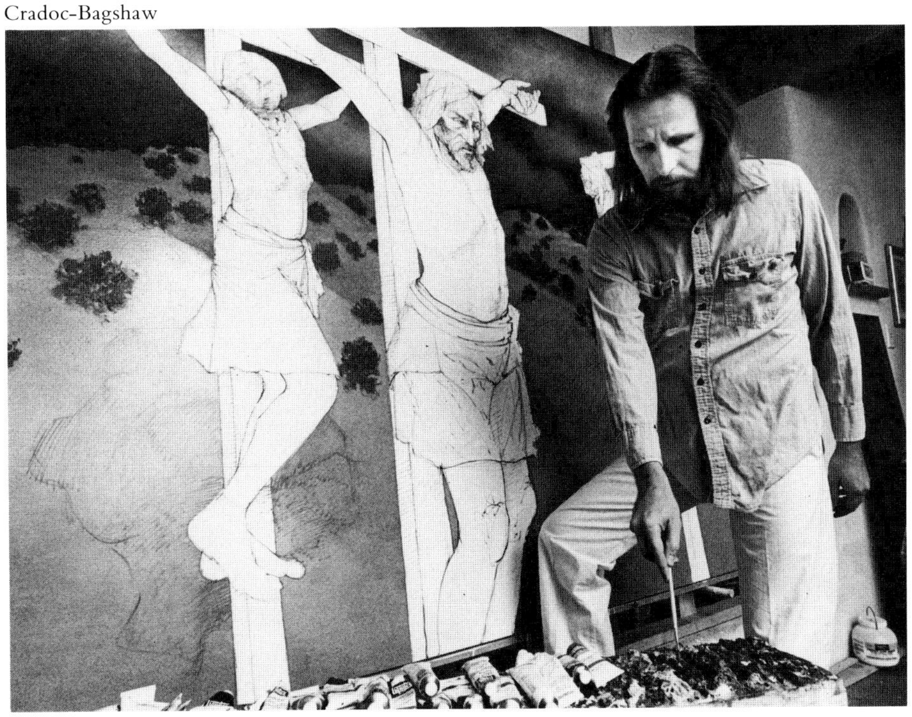

Pletka resumes work on his study of the Crucifixion.

New Mexican landscape. The arch of the backs is unmistakable. Without the color, tone, and texture of its creator, the complete statement of the painting is still a matter of conjecture to the observer. But one senses vintage Pletka, another thought-provoking observation of the human experience, this time using traditional Christianity and the Penitente theme as the analogue.

Pletka's personal pursuit of knowledge and the satisfaction he receives from the visual metaphors with which he portrays the similarities and connections of the life experience are only part of the story. In spite of his nonchalance about how his work is viewed by others and his determination not to succumb to commercial pressures and thus forsake his art, there is a quixotic irony: the need of others to perceive the extant connections of their heritage is just as great as Pletka's. So, although he often catches his audience unprepared and jars their complacency, no one views him passively. He is, almost unwittingly, a major purveyor of spiritual consanguinity.

His audience is widely diverse. Many of those who attend gallery showings are a surprise to Pletka. To his amazement, the average beholder will stare intently at his painting, glance fleetingly at the artist, and then retreat. "They might tell Nancy they like the painting, but they appear uncomfortable with my presence and usually say nothing to me," Pletka laments.

As to her role in the middle, Nancy comments, "I think they're too embarrassed to talk to Paul; they feel insecure about their impressions or judgments and aren't sure he'll be interested in their comments. It's too bad. Paul would genuinely enjoy their reinforcement."

There are other enthusiastic admirers whom Pletka never meets. The few Pletka paintings available each year are often sold before the last daubs of paint have dried, purchased on the basis of a transparency, a photograph on a gallery invitation, or a telephoned description.

Fondness for the elegance and beauty of his work prompted one of his collectors to buy *Roman Nose in Death, Slippery Eye,* and a series of bird lithographs: "I didn't buy them as investments; I didn't buy them to trade later. I bought them because I liked them. I enjoy staring at them. After I met Paul, what I found impressive was the great amount of research invested in these works. Hearing the stories about the paintings was just an added bonus. To me, he became a mentor of sorts, giving me suggestions of what to read and how to get past the grade-school preconceptions of what the Indians were. I learned that Paul is not painting the aboriginal. He's painting figures impacted upon by white culture. He's painting the termination of a sacred culture. What you see in these paintings is a transition.

"It's interesting to watch people react to the paintings in our home. The response ranges from immediate exclamation to dead silence. I presume some people don't like them and some are dumbfounded by the presence of the figures. Some are overcome by the emotional quality. There's a tremendous brooding about *Slippery Eye,* a pretty serious-looking guy who seems to be contemplating everything that ever went wrong in his life. Some people are more taken by the works after they hear the stories. They begin to appreciate the symbolism."

A staunch supporter who was not swept away by the artist's paintings when he first saw them in the mid-1970s gradually became devoted to the subject matter. Of buyers, he says, "People who want paintings that don't just quietly hang on the wall take to Pletka. If, however, they want something that does not challenge them, then Paul Pletka is not for them. Half the viewers fall into this category. 'How can anyone live with a thing like that?' they say. They find Pletka's art abhorrent. I think that perhaps Paul finally made peace with himself by not giving a damn what the public thinks. He is freely painting and expressing himself as he wishes, irrespective of whether the painting will sell. Because he has achieved commercial reinforcement, he has the self-assurance to do that."

One admirer began collecting Pletka's paintings in 1970. During the next decade, he and his wife bought several pieces, including four paintings that have been widely exhibited: *Talks to Gods, Cacique, Burial of Crazy Horse,* and *Eagle That Walks By the River No. II.* "There is a test we use in deciding what to collect. It's an emotional response. If the painting causes palpitations, buy it. There are other attractions in Paul's work, obviously. The meticulousness appeals to me. He far surpasses other so-called western artists, and I do not view his work in a regional context. Some people see his subject matter and execution as too strong. There is a certain element of grotesqueness in some of the paintings, but I don't see that as a problem. We live very comfortably with our Pletkas. His work is not easy to come by. There are many other paintings I would have been equally happy to have, but you have to be in the right place at the right time."

Another collector noticed Pletka's work in 1974 and arranged to buy a painting at a 1975 exhibit. "We had selected the painting we wanted from a brochure released before the show. We hired a guy to stand in line overnight. He got there about 2:00 in the morning and was second in line. When the doors opened at 3:00 the next afternoon, the first guy made a beeline for our painting, so our runner grabbed the next painting he saw. It was *Grandmother's Children,* and it's given us years of pleasure."

They bought other paintings, as well as watercolors and lithographs, and are convinced that Pletka's superlative lithographs are paragons of the medium: "His bird lithographs are perhaps the finest that have been done in this country. Period. That's a big statement. I'm sure you can arouse a good argument about who's best in the medium, but I think anyone familiar with Paul's work would admit he's a forerunner in the field."

The owner of *Ceremonial Bird Wands,* the mixed

media *Jicarilla,* and the watercolor *Albino Deer Head,* comments, "Paul's paintings strike me emotionally, like a slap across the face. Incredible force. When other people see them, they are fascinated. The paintings always evoke comments. Some people go wild and others don't like them one bit. There's no middle ground, just extremes in either direction. Nobody is doing what Paul does. No one comes close. His work bears a distinct personality you can recognize in the dark."

Pletka cringes when criticized, fidgets when extolled, but neither form of feedback infiltrates his canvas. When at work, he turns his back on detractors and aficionados alike, though he concedes his position as an artist-in-demand is luxurious: "I've been granted special privileges in society that many people are denied. I have freedom to move at will. My eccentricities are indulged. I feel, then, an obligation to repay these liberties. One way I do that is to reach for the highest quality—the finest outpouring—within the limits of my capability."

Metaphors, Analogues, and Posterity

Painting is not an aesthetic operation; it's a form of magic designed as a mediator between this strange hostile world and us . . . giving form to our terrors as well as our desires.

Pablo Picasso

It is an elusive quality—unpredictable and impossible to contain within boundaries. Outsiders, looking in, have labeled it the creative process and only an elite few have ever discovered its legerdemain. Paul Pletka is numbered among those who manifest its influence.

His appeal has the tenor of universality. He is admired by an eclectic audience: The realist looks at Pletka's paintings and sees Indians or western Americana. The ethnologist reveres Pletka's knowledge and detailed treatment of artifacts, customs, and ceremony from bygone cultures. His painterly skills astound many; his audacity enchants some and overpowers others. Yet everyone knows at a visceral level that the Pletka statement transcends simple interpretation.

Pletka addresses magic and metamorphism—he is a neo-surrealist, a painter of visual irony.

With his art he investigates less well-known beliefs and customs adopted by other cultures to explain the mysterious. He brings into focus the relentless efforts of each human generation to make sense of, to find rationality in, those elements of nature so powerful that they exert influence beyond the realm of human control. He suggests a way of looking at the world that is essentially spiritual. He uses the visual image as a metaphor for a philosophical camouflage in nature that obscures the harmony among all forces of life.

It is to his credit that the extant subject matter of his canvas represents known quantities and environments. It is a time-honored component of effective persuasion and tutelage to launch the student from familiar ground, moving from the known to those vistas yet to be known.

Pletka encourages a direct confrontation with the unknown. *Las Muertas* invites a contemplation of death without the shackles of constraint or fear. Paradoxically, it suggests that evasion of mystic considerations is not logical. "Death is only one of several universals that we refuse to recognize as part of the human picture," he says. "Cultural idiosyncrasies constrain our ability to accept and deal with what is really no more than the shared experience."

These universals and the concomitant search they engender for ways to describe the unknown dominate his work.

He portrays the commonality of people since the beginning of recorded history who, when unable to rationally describe certain life forces, develop mystical explanations or religions to guide them. Commitment and sacrifice for the good of the family or community, for instance as expressed in *Sun Dance,* is an accepted modern concept. The means by which these people of the upper Missouri River sought to accomplish this dedication to others may, however, appear strange or aberrant to the modern eye.

Takes Back Twice tells the tale of the Crow medicine bundles. Skulls of wise or clairvoyant people were preserved and thus perceived to be available for regular consultation. They are said to have provided valuable responses to queries such as: "Will this be a good day? Will I succeed in finding horses for the village today?" The skull-head of the figure in the painting is interpretive of this belief and exemplifies Pletka's use of visual irony. He raises for our consideration the fact that the skull need not connote a negative image. In the context of his painting, it signifies a positive influence of well-being.

"The sand lizard umbilical fetish, the horned water monster, and the metamorphosed central character all have meaning far beyond their simply physical presence," Pletka explains. "They represent the expression of spiritual entity—calling to mind the correspondences of all states of being."

Although recognizing the variation of content and ritual, he senses the unerring thread of sameness . . . a belief that behind all motivating forces lies a similar spiritual presence—a shared spirituality that makes everything work. He suggests a reassessment of values, or at least a greater openness to experiences of the past. "Our unwillingness to gain insight from the past confounds me," Pletka says. "There is a curious kind of comfort in knowing that we are in fact the torch bearers for the spiritual understanding that unites the past to the future. I don't mean to set myself up as someone who sees more or knows more than others," he continues, "but I am intrigued by the habits of history and particularly with those elements that seem occult to modern eyes. I wonder what will be said of our society some day. Will the people of the twenty-second century view our customs with an understanding of our role in the development of their cultural patterns? Will they recognize us as their ancestors—as having contributed to the body of knowledge that marks their way of life? Will our spiritual brotherhood and sisterhood survive the transit of time and events?"

Pletka has come to this conviction over time. The late 1970s and early 1980s have witnessed an extraordinary refinement in both his skills as a painter and in the depth of his perspective. But what of the years ahead; what is Pletka's view to the future?

"I have no solid answers," he says. "Although I have a fairly good idea, great ideas can always sidetrack me." He plans to continue his series on the Hispanics, exploring their relationship to Indians and to the Southwest. He would like to find time to try his hand at sculpture. He states unequivocally that he will never stop painting Indians.

New horizons also beckon and intrigue the enigmatic Pletka as he contemplates his future. He is quick to point out that he moves slowly into new directions, is never bold or direct, preferring instead a measured and purposeful approach. "If I were prone to conjecture, I would guess that the Peruvian Head Cult might someday be the subject of some of my work." His eyes alive with excitement, Pletka articulates results of the assiduous research for which he is known. "I'm fascinated by the fact that such a highly developed society could be so easily obliterated under such amoral circumstances. A flourishing and very beautiful people were ruined as the conquistadors and Christian dogma swept through like a tornado. The Trophy Head Cult was a significant feature of this historic culture. Their iconography is replete with little men holding heads that look like cartoons—but they're real heads. A whole religion grew out of this custom."

Evidence of the trophy head custom in the mound-building societies of the lower Mississippi River Valley and the Fremont culture of Utah deepened Pletka's interest. "It might have permeated the whole western hemisphere at one time. I'm interested for purely anthropological reasons and in the opportunity to examine the juxtaposition of that cult and Christianity."

He describes his attraction to the Masai of Africa as a chance to go back in history. "I have a suspicion that the warrior society of the Masai bears a high correlation to the Hidatsa and Mandans in 1850. Even though they are receiving an education that espouses a modern, occidental way of life, the Masai fiercely protect their beliefs and territory. The Kenyan government has not been able to dislodge them. Their cultural milieu is described as markedly similar to that of the American Indian before the advent of the white man." Although he characterizes himself as primarily a studio painter, he will go to Africa if he can.

Pletka is an explorer of visually uncharted waters, searching the magic and mysticism of the human experience. In Socratic mode he uses his canvas to doubt and question, to elicit clear expression of universal truths. Pletka's paintings are his progeny, his contribution to the archival history of the planet. He contemplates the age-old wonderings of what and when and why and gives substance to our fears and longings. He illuminates the dark corners—giving us dimension and beauty.

He has studied the past and senses the future. Paul Pletka is a visionary oracle of our times.

Retrospective

. . . The painting is life . . . will possess no more love than you possess, show no more bewilderment than you betray, be no more sincere than you are, create no more awe than is felt by you. In essence, the painting is an astigmatized portrayal of you. It is your Rorschach with id and plaster cast. It can be no better than you are. It is essential that we give of the whole and not of the part, for the picture is our legacy left by tomorrow's dead for tomorrow's living.

IVAN LE LORRAINE ALBRIGHT

Roman Nose in Death
1974
Acrylic on linen canvas
84 x 72

Ice, a Cheyenne medicine man also known as White Bull, had a dream about Thunder, one of the beings of the sky. Thunder prescribed to Ice an elaborate headdress rich with powerful medicine, and Ice made the headdress for Roman Nose, the famous Elk Horn scraper man. The powerful war bonnet trailed to the ground with a double stream of eagle feathers, red on one side, white on the other. Because the headdress was Thunder's own, a special paint of lightning was required. Therefore, charcoal scraped from a tree struck by lightning was applied to Roman Nose's body. The single horn is a phallic symbol representing strength and fertility. Sundry talismans worn by Roman Nose to protect him in battle include the kingfisher—a bullet-proofer—and a bat believed to endow the wearer with swiftness. Yellow hail spots, designed to conjure weather foul enough to deter the enemy, have been applied, and Roman Nose's shield is painted red, the sacred color. The heron, not necessarily among Roman Nose's medicine charms, was added to balance the composition.

Pletka says, "The historical material is prominent, but it's not the main objective in the painting. I would never compromise the aesthetic value for historical accuracy."

Roman Nose, his face seeming to dissolve, clutches his chest after a bullet pierces his spine. The war medicine has failed, perhaps because the warrior ignored one of the taboos associated with his awesome headdress. As with the laws governing the contrary societies, Roman Nose could not consume any food that had been touched by a metal implement. On the day before the battle in which he was to be killed, Roman Nose ate bread lifted from a skillet with a metal fork. It was served to him by a woman; thus the elk tooth shroud in the painting. Roman Nose was killed the next day at the Ari Karee fork of the Republican River.

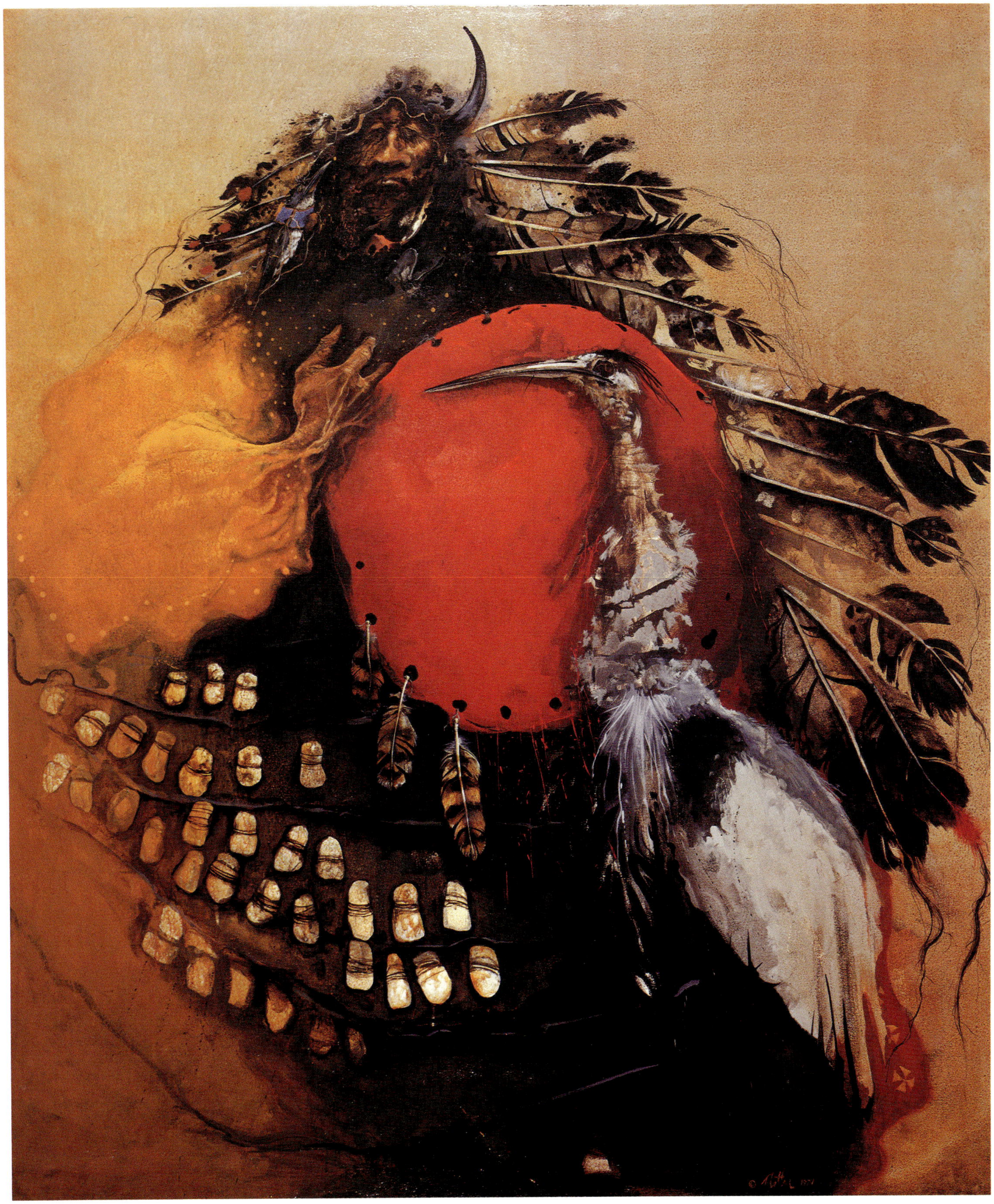

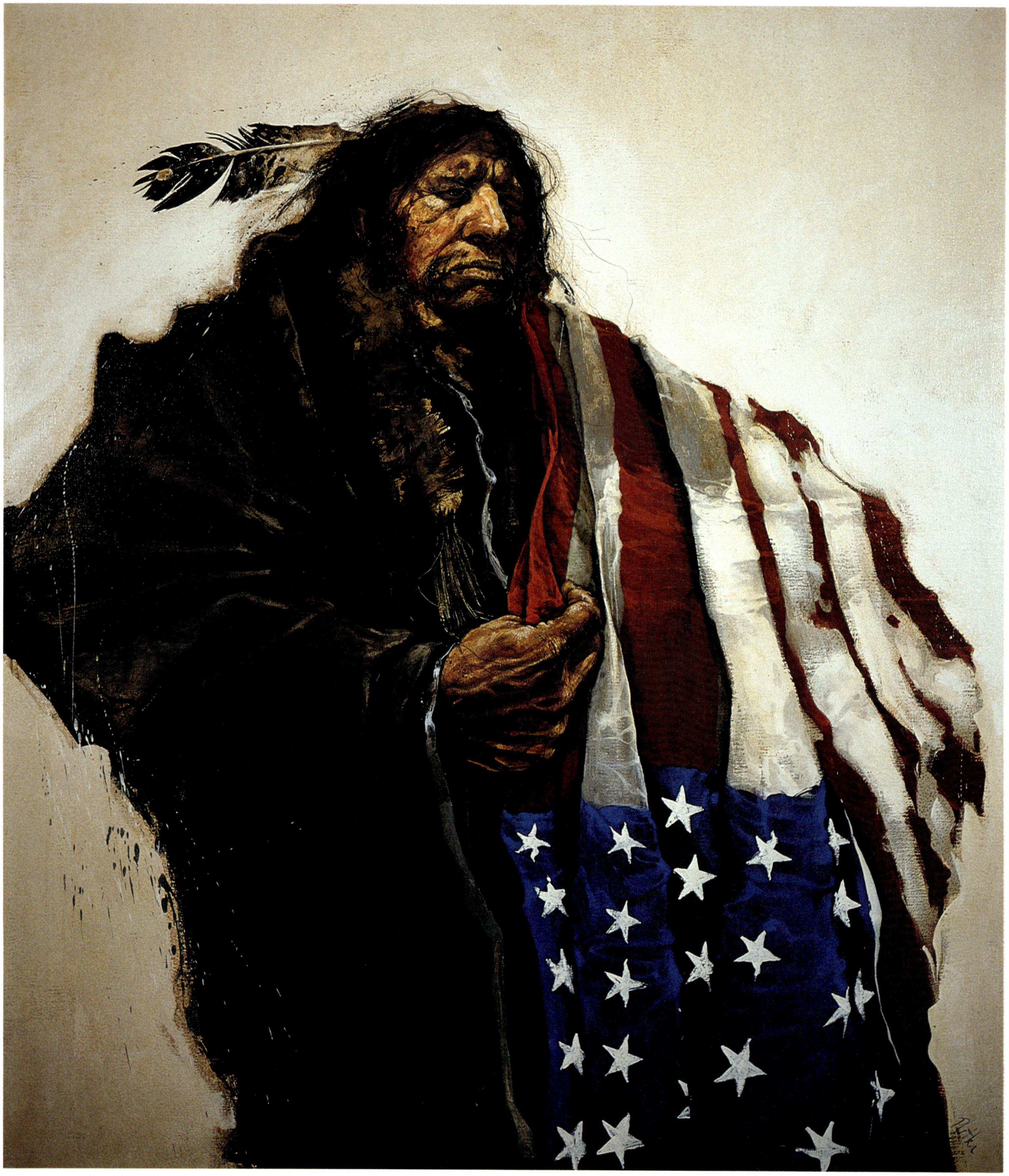

Nota 'A
1974
Acrylic on linen canvas
54 x 48

Nota 'A is a self-portrait of the artist portraying Charles Buck, or Buckskin Charlie, a renowned Ute chief. U.S. Government authorities commonly gave canes, peace medals, or in this case an American flag, to Indian leaders. Some chiefs wore them as an outward display of patriotism, others because they found the colorful composition an attractive garment. Pletka painted the portrait as a joke, never intending to sell it. But his dealer insisted the painting was Pletka's best effort that year, and the portrait was quickly sold.

Red Lodge
1974
Acrylic on linen canvas
20 x 30

Red Lodge was painted to depict a deserted Blackfoot camp. Though Pletka's portrayals of tepees often are luminous and flaunting, this scene is tinged with a brooding sky and uncomfortable hollowness that quietly remarks on a tragedy—decimation by disease.

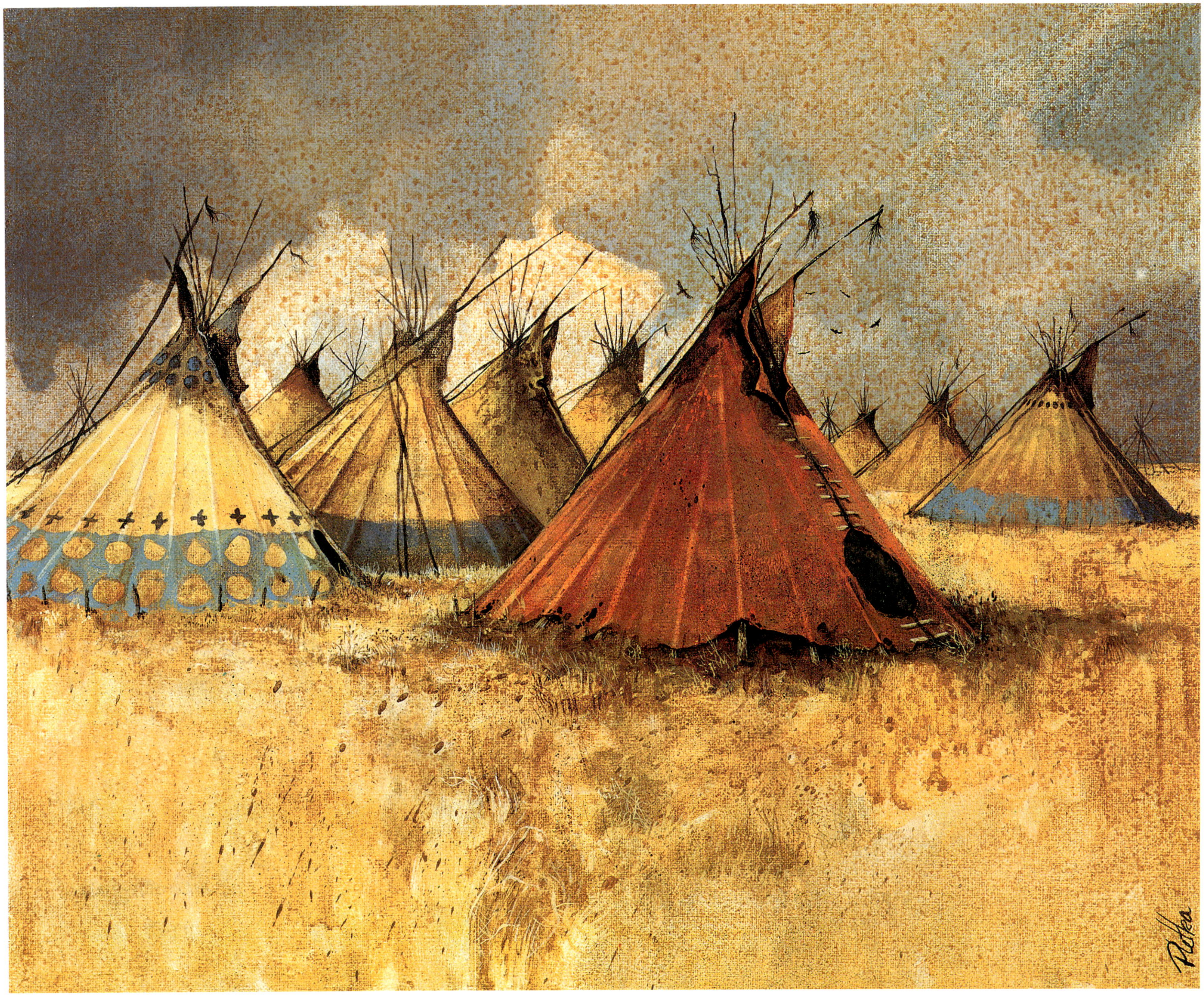

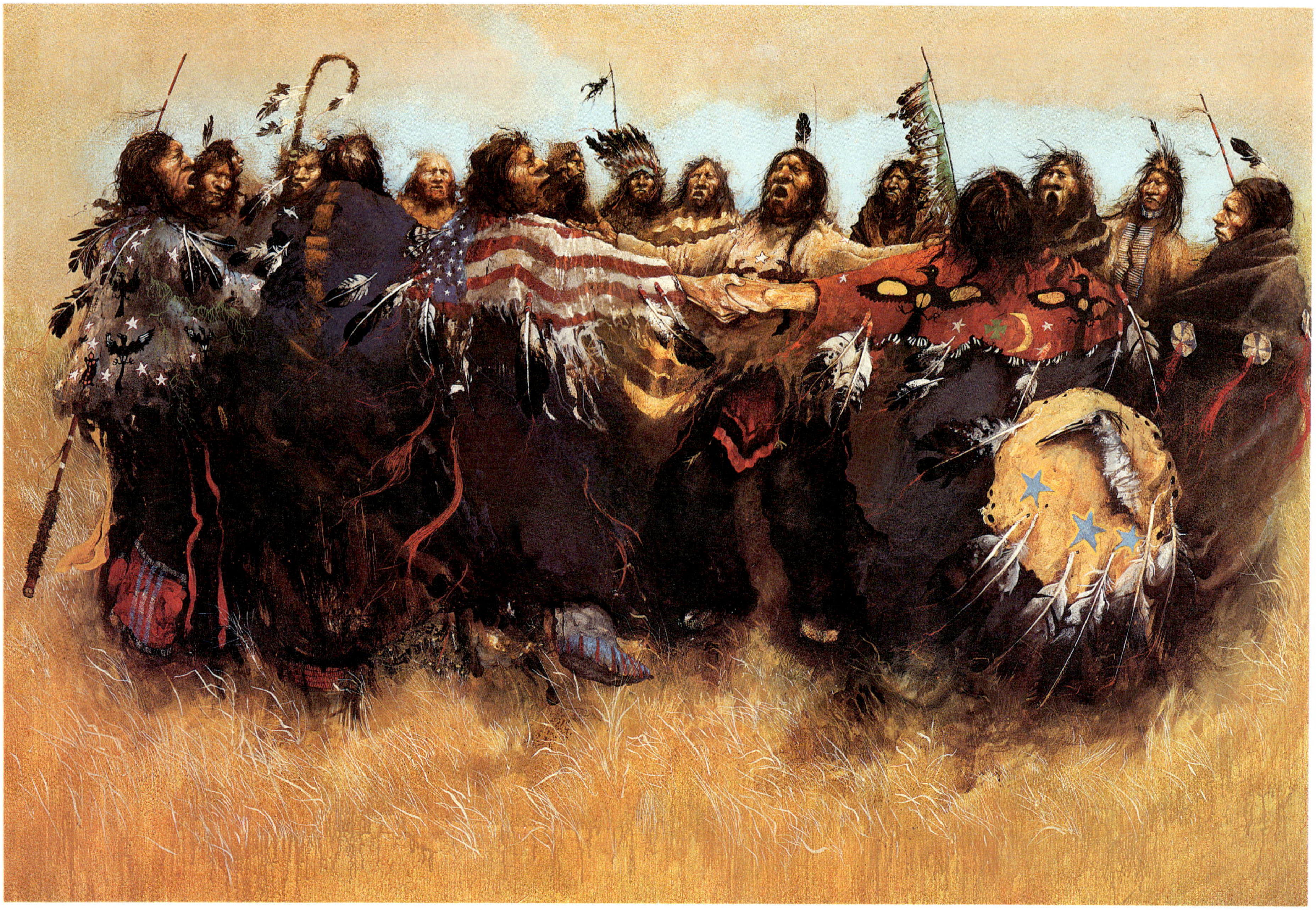

Ghost Dance
1974
Acrylic on linen canvas
48 x 72

Wovoka, a Paiute prophet, founded the Ghost Dance religion that swept across the Plains in the 1880s, inspiring a new wave of hope for return to the old ways of prosperity and freedom. The ritual included frantic, ceaseless dancing and singing that often led to trances and fainting spells. The religion embraced nonviolence and passivity. Believers felt assured the rites would bring back the great herds of buffalo and ghosts of the ancestors, as well as rid the land of white men.

"It was a last measure," Pletka said, "an act of total desperation. This is the first painting I ever did of a Ghost Dance. I think it may have been my first successful multi-figure picture. At that point, I was trying to work in mass, so most of the pictures were concerned with large monumental masses. This one includes all kinds of Ghost Dance imagery, a kind of potpourri representing the people involved in the movement. There's an Arapaho shirt on the left and a Sioux shirt on the figure with his arms outstretched. Ghost Dance iconography has a lot to do with celestial symbols like the stars and moon on the shirt with the magpies."

"My children, my children
Look! The earth is about to move,
Look! The earth is about to move.
My father tells me so,
My father tells me so."
—Ghost Dance Song

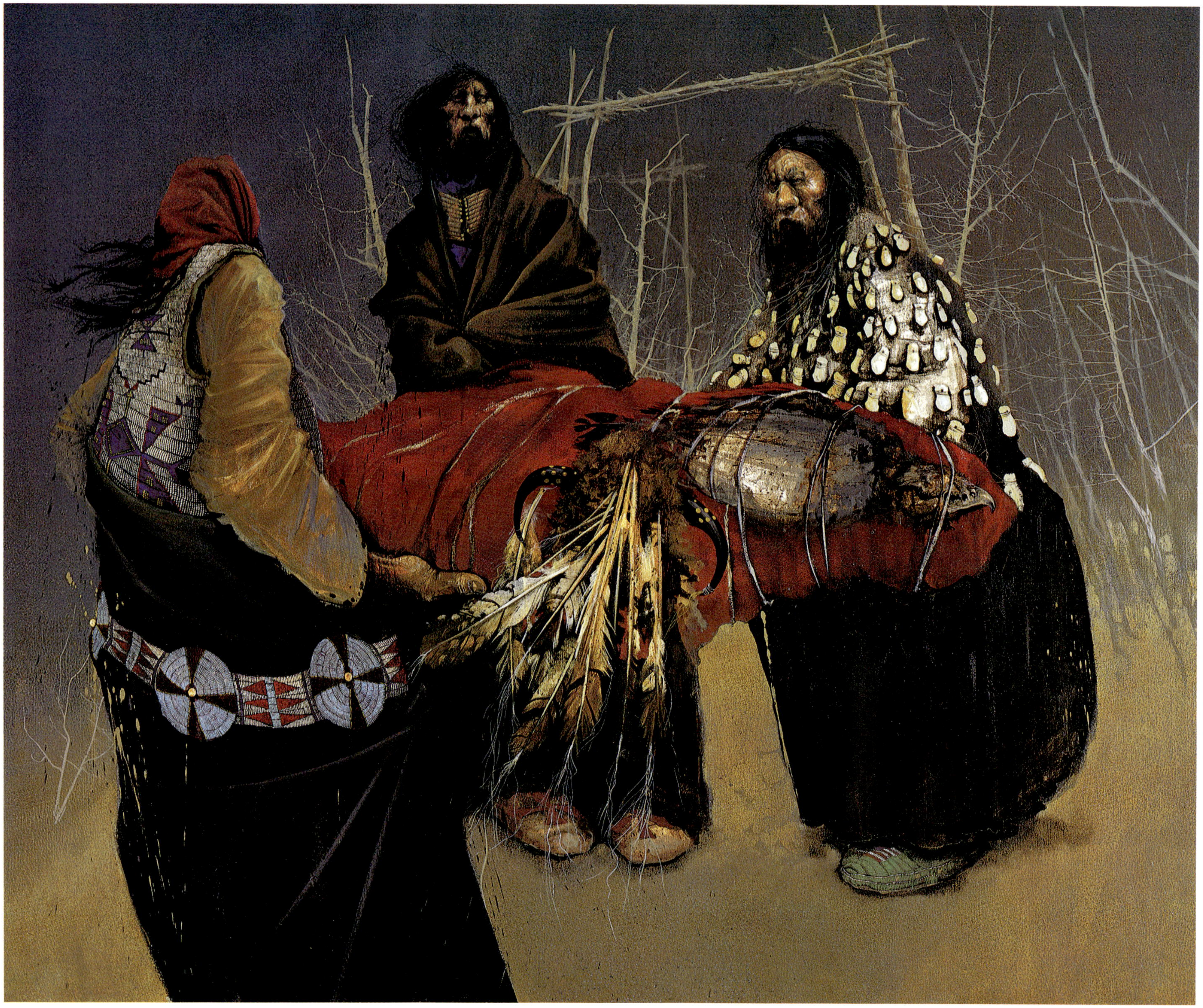

Burial of Crazy Horse
1974
Acrylic on linen canvas
48 x 60

Crazy Horse, famous chief of the Oglala Sioux and nephew of Spotted Tail, "The Orator" of the Brulé Sioux, was stabbed to death September 5, 1877, at Fort Robinson, Nebraska. The next morning, soldiers presented the body to Crazy Horse's mother and father, who carried the body to Spotted Tail Agency and placed it on a scaffold. They were accompanied by Touch-the-Clouds, who is portrayed as the middle figure in the painting. He is flanked by the father of Crazy Horse on the left and the dead chief's mother, who wears an elk-tooth dress. The bonnet of Crazy Horse is patterned after the original, housed at the Museum of the American Indian, Heye Foundation, in New York City. The parents of Crazy Horse buried their son near Wounded Knee Creek, though the grave's location has never been found.

Rain Crows
1974
Acrylic on linen canvas
42 x 60

This painting depicts the Snake priest, who participates in the Hopi Snake Dance, a supplication for rain.

Most of the information behind Pletka's paintings comes from research, but this one was done intuitively. He didn't know much about the Hopis and was not aware that these headdresses should be composed of dyed eagle breast and piñon jay feathers. The jays have been shown here in a living state, put in because, in the back of his mind, he thought they belonged there. He found out later that indeed they should have been there.

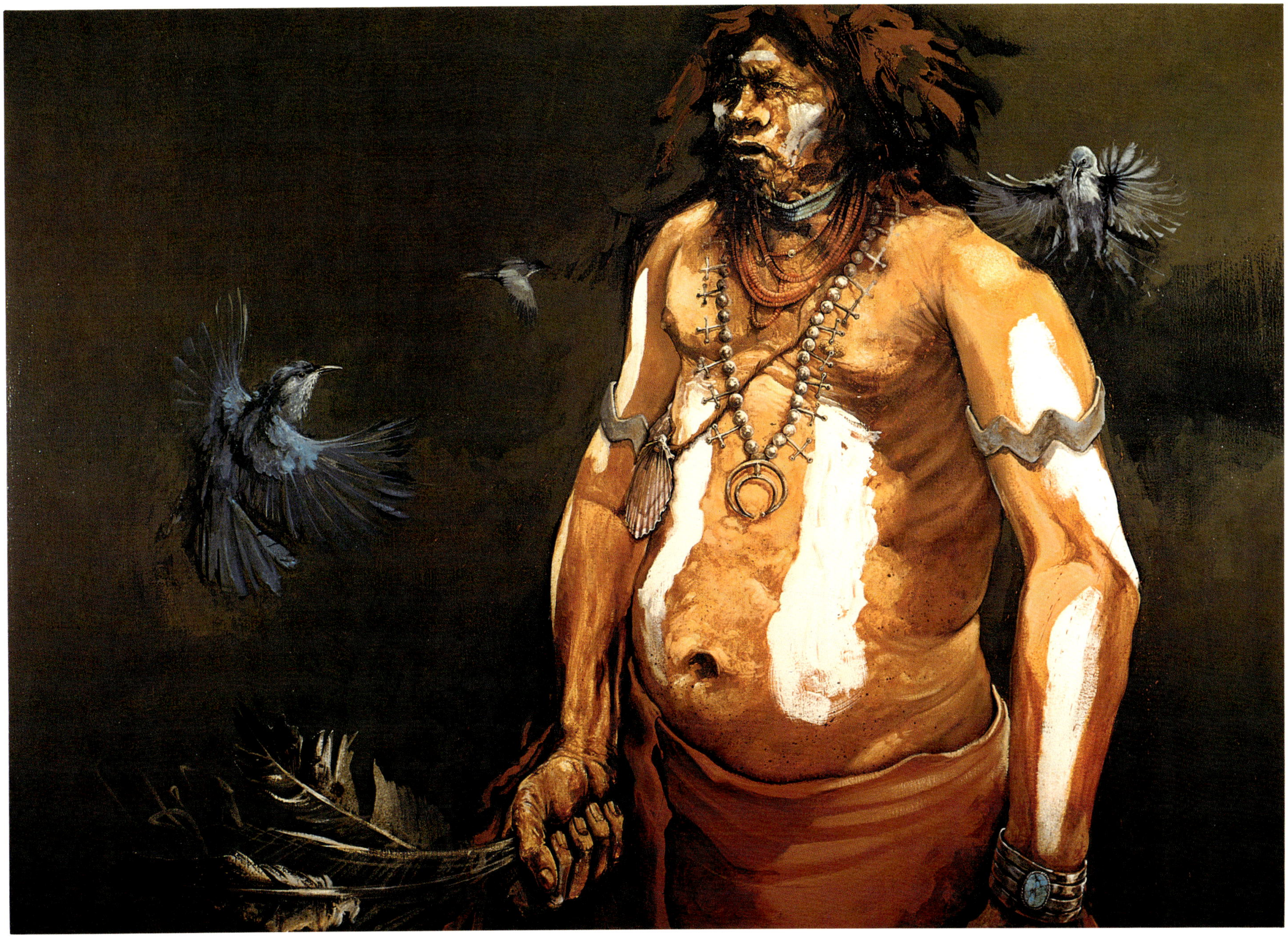

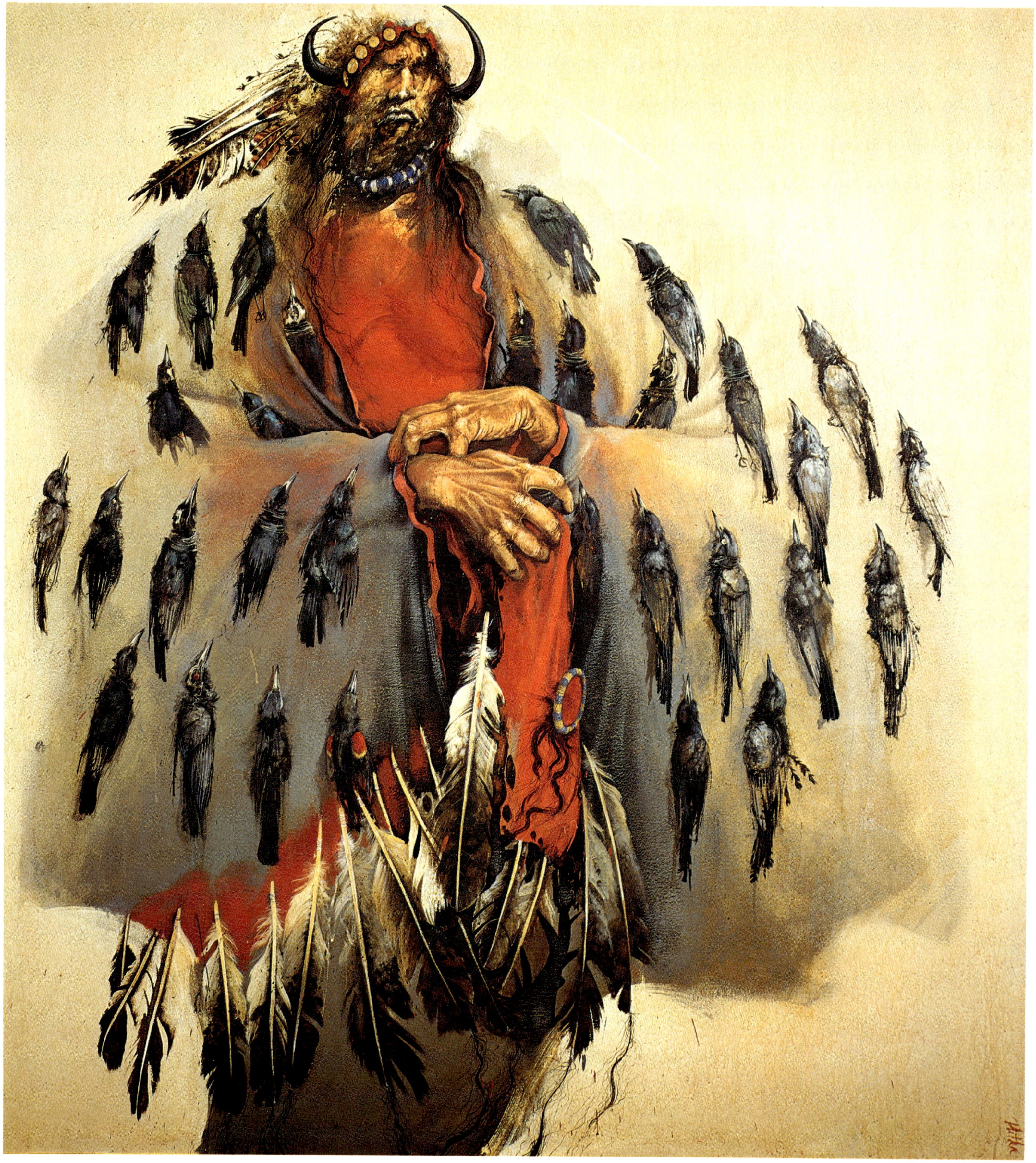

Bacu Sua
1975
Acrylic on linen canvas
72 x 66

This Crow Indian is a member of the Blackbird branch of the Strawberries, a Bacu Sua, translated from Crow to mean "tobacco society." The Crow Indians did not engage in the sacrificial bloodletting of their Plains neighbors, but the tobacco-planting renewal ceremony was a philosophical parallel to the Sun Dance. The society acknowledged the onset of spring and celebrated fertility. Pletka's fanciful rendering of a Bacu Sua member depicts a prescribed robe adorned with stuffed blackbirds.

The Horse Thief
1975
Acrylic on linen canvas
42 x 54

This painting is the result of a Pletka nightmare, in which he was a settler killed by an Indian who bashed his skull in with a rifle butt. *The Horse Thief* figure looks like that man. The carved wooden horse around his neck is a war talisman, like a Horse Dance stick, usually representative of a favorite war horse or stolen horse. Stealing horses was an honorable activity among Plains Indians. Typically, the carvings were decorated with horse hair or feathers, such as those used for the tail. The Northern Plains warrior shirt has hail spots and strands of horse hair, a rather plainly decorated old man shirt. A yellow-headed blackbird is fastened to his braid.

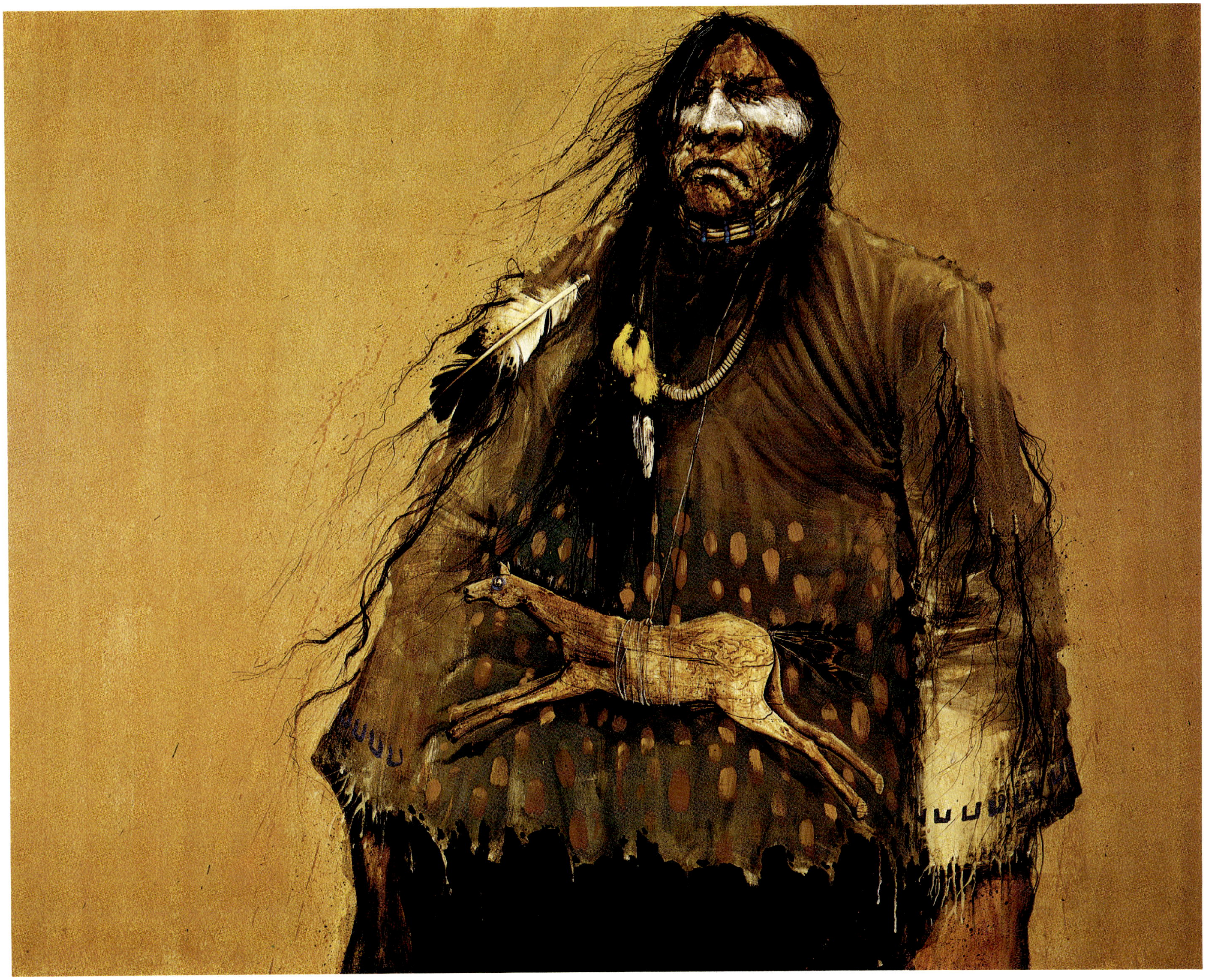

Crow Indian
1975
Acrylic on linen canvas
48 x 60

Historians reason that the Crows survived as a tribe because they cooperated with the government during the Indian Wars of the late nineteenth century. A few wise men among them realized there was no use fighting the overwhelming tide of Anglo humanity. Along with some Shoshones, they were enlisted as scouts, thereby managing to keep small portions of their homeland without being moved about too much; the Crow reservation is still located in Montana. The Crow Indian in this painting displays a potpourri of war emblems, including a warrior narrative drawn across his old robe adorned with pony beads. The American flag painted on his face is Pletka's indication he is a scout. The gear on his head includes a horned medicine bonnet. A war whistle is affixed to the crow on his robe.

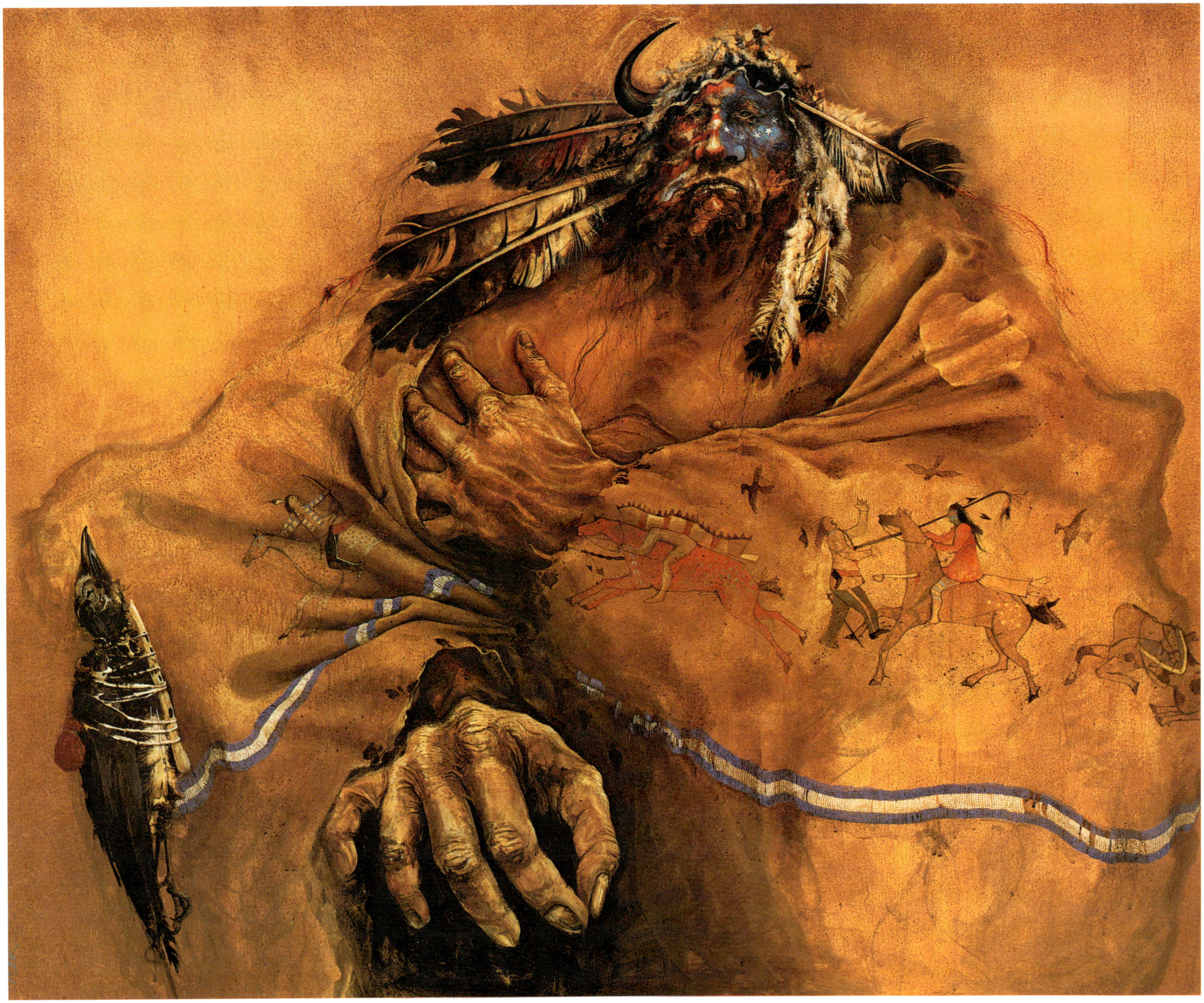

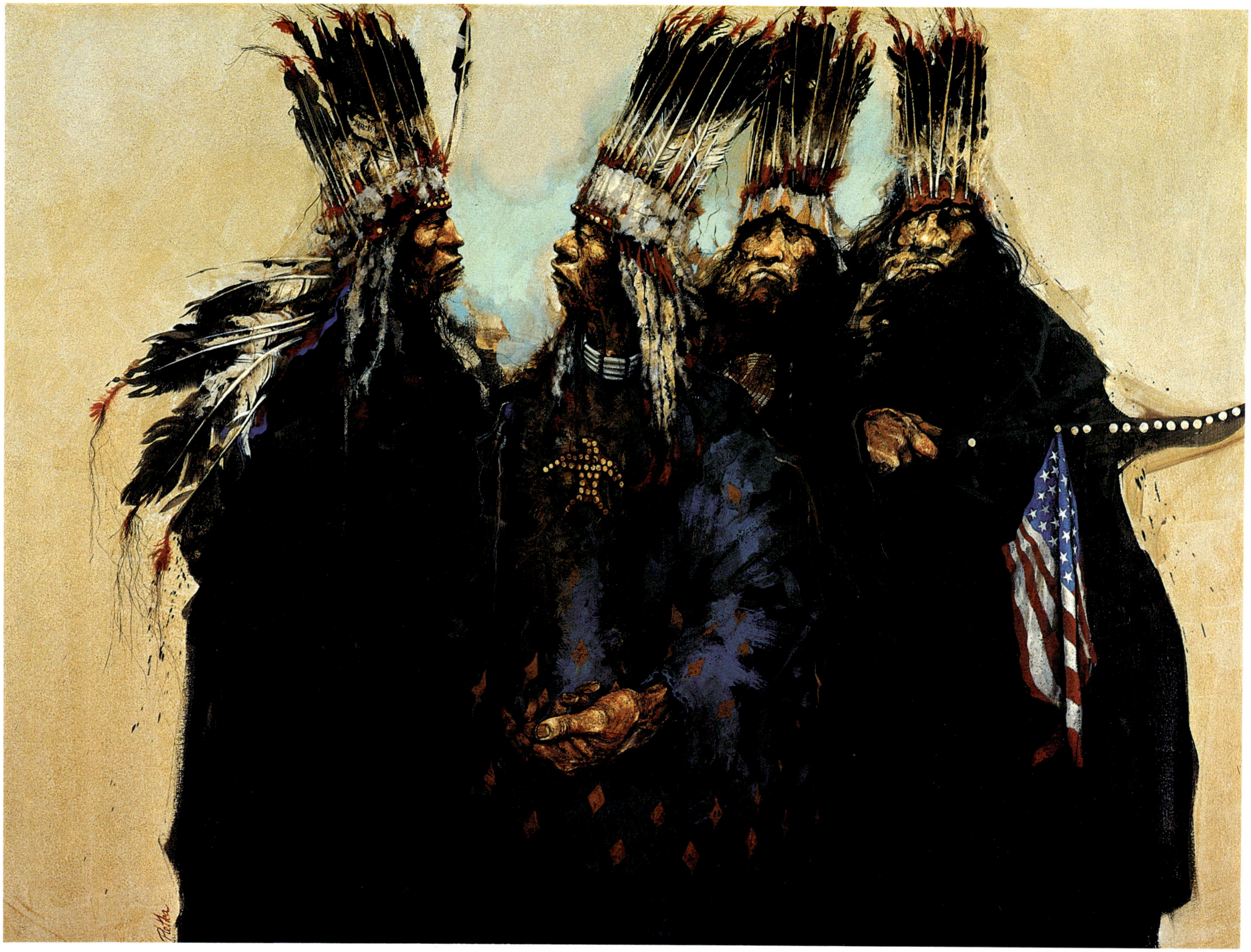

All the King's Men
1975
Acrylic on linen canvas
48 x 66

The erect headdresses of the southern Blackfoot reminded Pletka of the opulent crowns of Renaissance royalty, hence the title from the *Humpty Dumpty* nursery rhyme. The man with the flag attached to his coup stick is not likely an American patriot. Bunting was routinely distributed and especially abundant in election years, and Indians admired its colors and design. The blue shirt is studded with polliwogs, representing renewal and fertility. Tribe members were extremely fond of pheasant hackles dyed commercially or with Chinese vermilion, and they cherished ermine tails, which are affixed to the bonnets in this case.

All the King's Men illustrates Pletka's phase of distorting faces. Stretched and drooping, the faces appear more as masks than flesh, a technique employed to connote a psychological breakdown of identity.

Oldest Whose Ears Hang Backward
1975
Acrylic on linen canvas
54 x 72

This painting depicts the legend of two brave warriors who, before they went to war against each other, were eagle brothers. According to Hidatsa Indian Wolf Chief, the Rocky Mountain eagles so loved the Indians that they became men and joined two tribes, Hidatsa and Shiwahuwa, in hopes of helping them. They both grew up to become holy men, but did not continue their friendship, since the two tribes were at war. Each eagle-man believed his to be the superior lifestyle, and each resolved to slay the other and bring his skull to abide in a better homeland.

Later, a battle commenced on the Knife River, and the Shiwahuwa were defeated. The Hidatsa arrows, however, could not penetrate the flesh of one warrior guarding his tribe's retreat. The Hidatsa eagle-man touched his medicine pipe to the lips of his warrior brother, who shivered and died. The Hidatsa cut off the Shiwahuwa's head.

Wolf Chief described the ensuing events as follows:

"The Hidatsa brought home his friend's head and cleaned the skull, and when it was dry took it into his lodge. In the skull he made his medicine; it was hanging on the wall, neatly covered with robes, and it was always treated with honor.

"When the Hidatsa became old, he put an aromatic herb (pennyroyal) in a bowl of water until it was sweet-smelling; he drank of the water and rubbed it over his body, and became a young man again. But when he grew old a second time, he said, 'I am tired of living among men. I want to go back whence I came. I long to live again with my friend as I did before I entered this present life.' "

He called together his tribe, informed them of his impending death and instructed them to prepare his skull to hang beside that of his brother.

The Hidatsa eagle-man, according to Wolf Chief, said: "Now I die here. But before I die, I make you a promise. My skull and my friend's skull shall be the medicines of my band. . . . You shall choose a trustworthy man to be keeper-of-the-skulls, and he shall keep them in his lodge. And so long as my skull is thus kept in honor, my spirit will remain with it to help the people and be their guide."

Oldest Whose Ears Hang Backward depicts the keeper-of-the-skulls and the reunited eagle brothers.

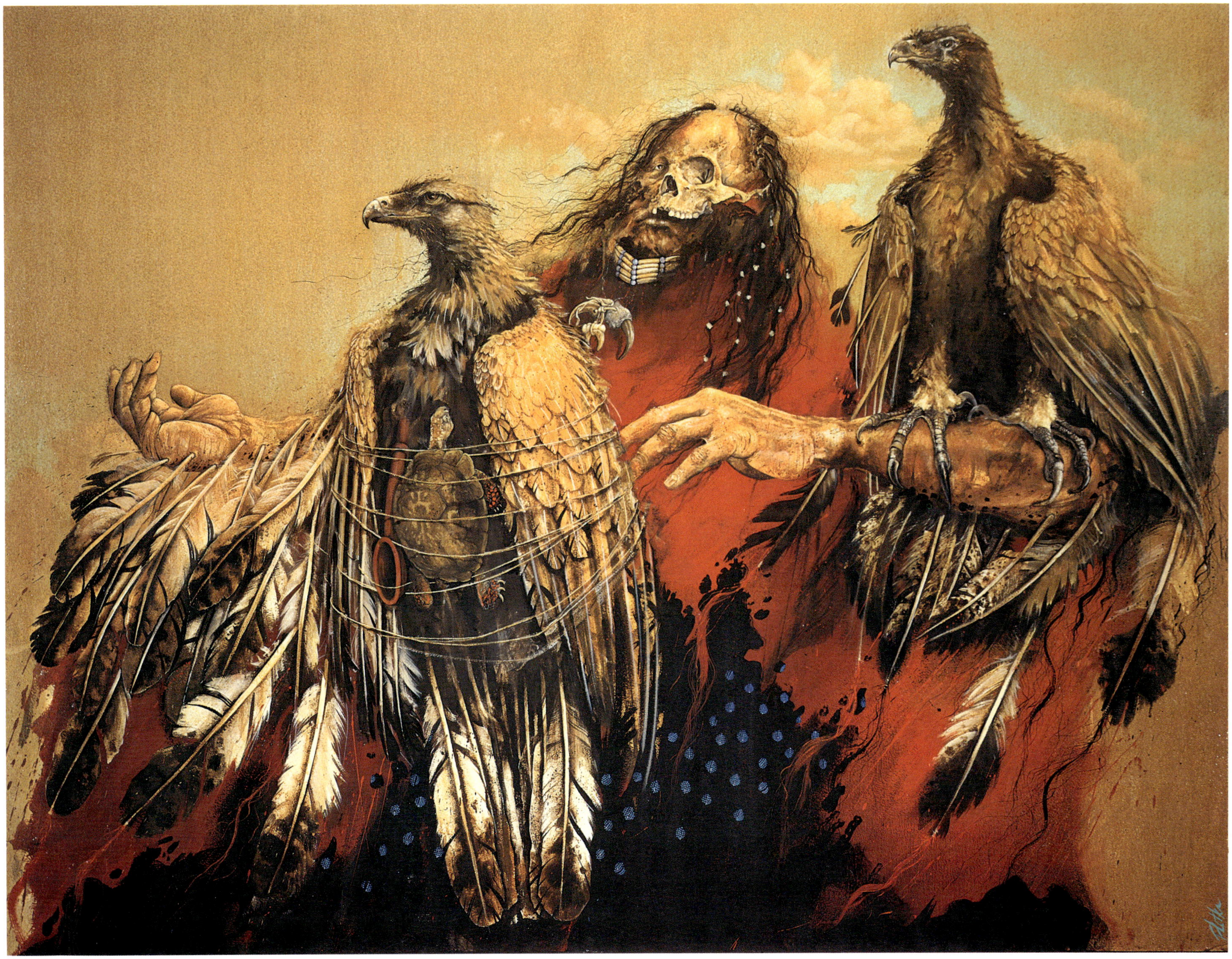

Sings to the Wind
1975
Acrylic on linen canvas
48 x 60

A Sioux warrior is depicted wearing two artifacts Pletka once owned, a war shirt and shield. The shirt had deteriorated beyond repair since its construction in the 1890s, and the artist resolved to document the once-glorious garment in a painting. He used the figure as a mannequin to flaunt two time-spoiled vestiges of the Plains warrior's heyday.

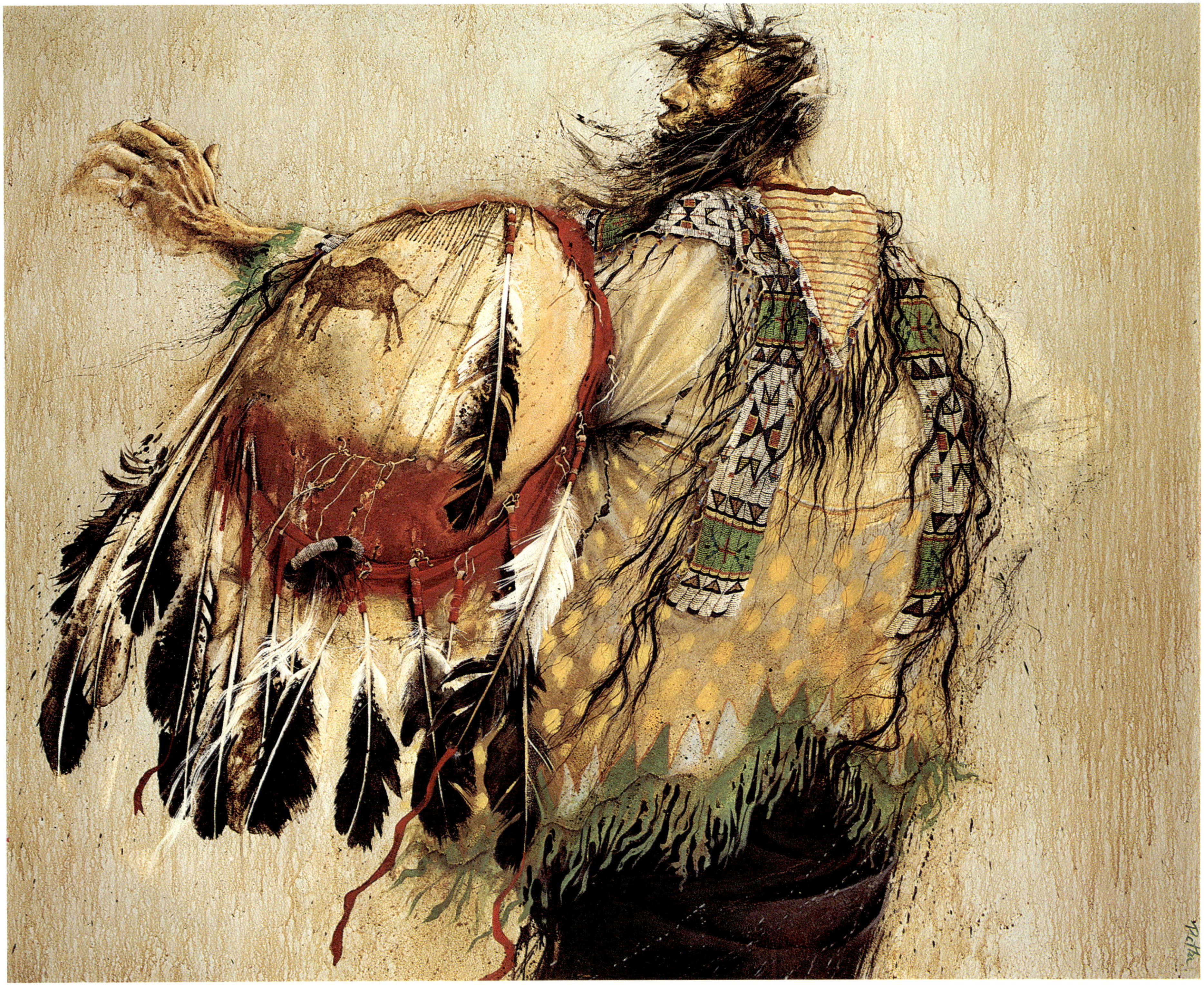

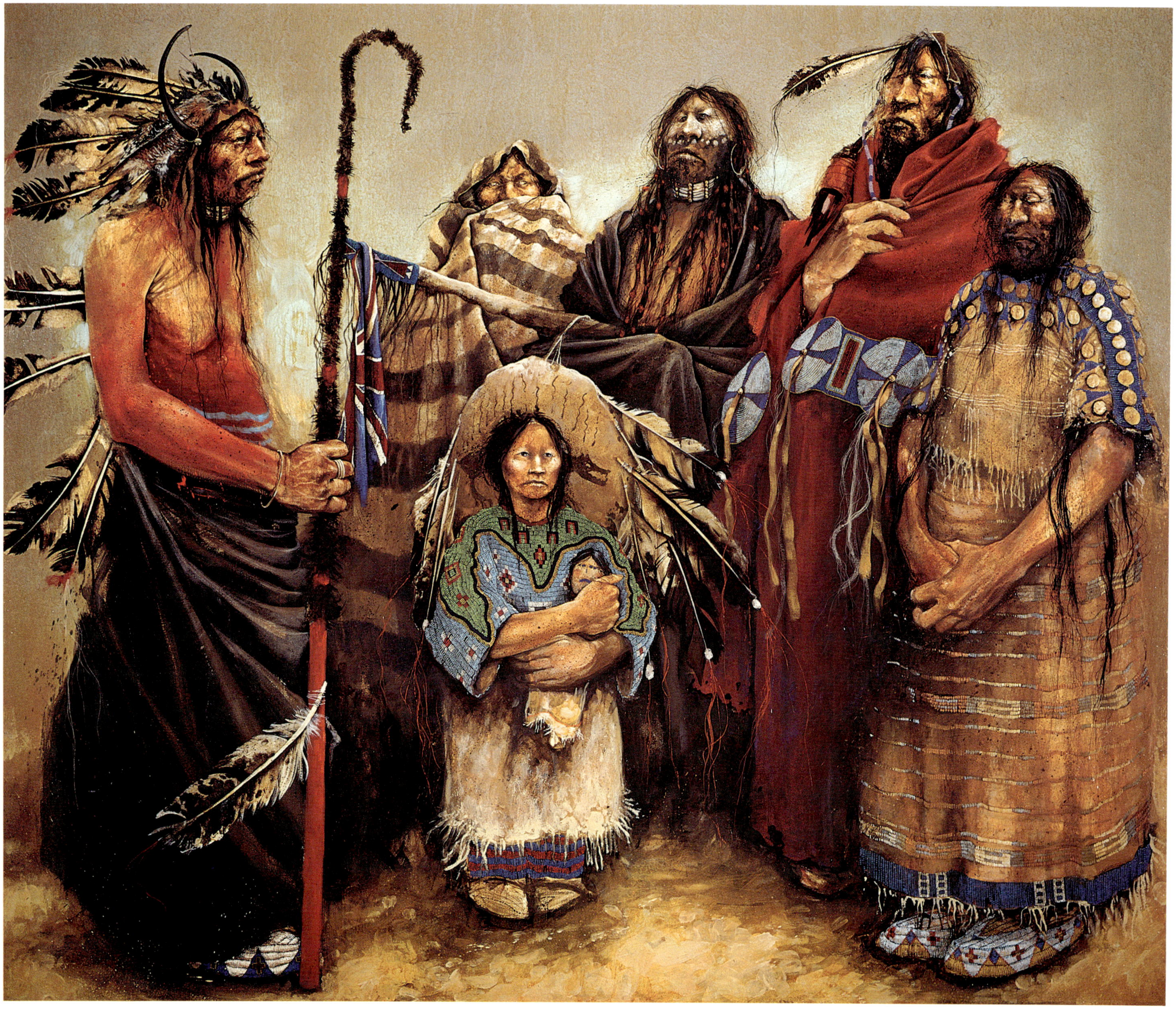

Grandmother's Children
1975
Acrylic on linen canvas
60 x 72

This grouping depicts a family of Assiniboin Indians, called Grandmother's children because they live in Grandmother's land, Canada. In the late nineteenth century, the tribe was concentrated north of Montana and North Dakota. Customary garb of the Assiniboin paralleled the dress of the Mandan, Hidatsa, and Blackfoot Indians. The old woman at far right wears a two-piece Cree dress patterned after one acquired during the Lewis and Clark expedition of the early 1800s. Next to her, a man in a Hudson Bay blanket wears a beaded blanket strip of typical Assiniboin production. The third figure from the right has decorated his rifle case with a Canadian flag, and his shield portrays a bear, considered powerful medicine. Traditionally, military society members would append to their headdresses protective talismans derived from sacred dreams. The warrior on the left carries a hawk in his horned bonnet. The figure behind the little girl clutching the doll is shrouded in a valuable first phase Navajo chief blanket.

Skin Walker
1975
Acrylic on linen canvas
54 x 48

Skin Walker is slang for Coyote Man or Wolf Man, an entity of an occult belief still prevalent on the Navajo reservation. Nobody knows much about these men, but it's rumored they are capable of transmuting into coyotes that roam the roadsides at night. The Skin Walker in this painting wears a turquoise earring, a Navajo element. His hands are clasped in supplication, and if one looks closely, two ears are growing from the top of his head.

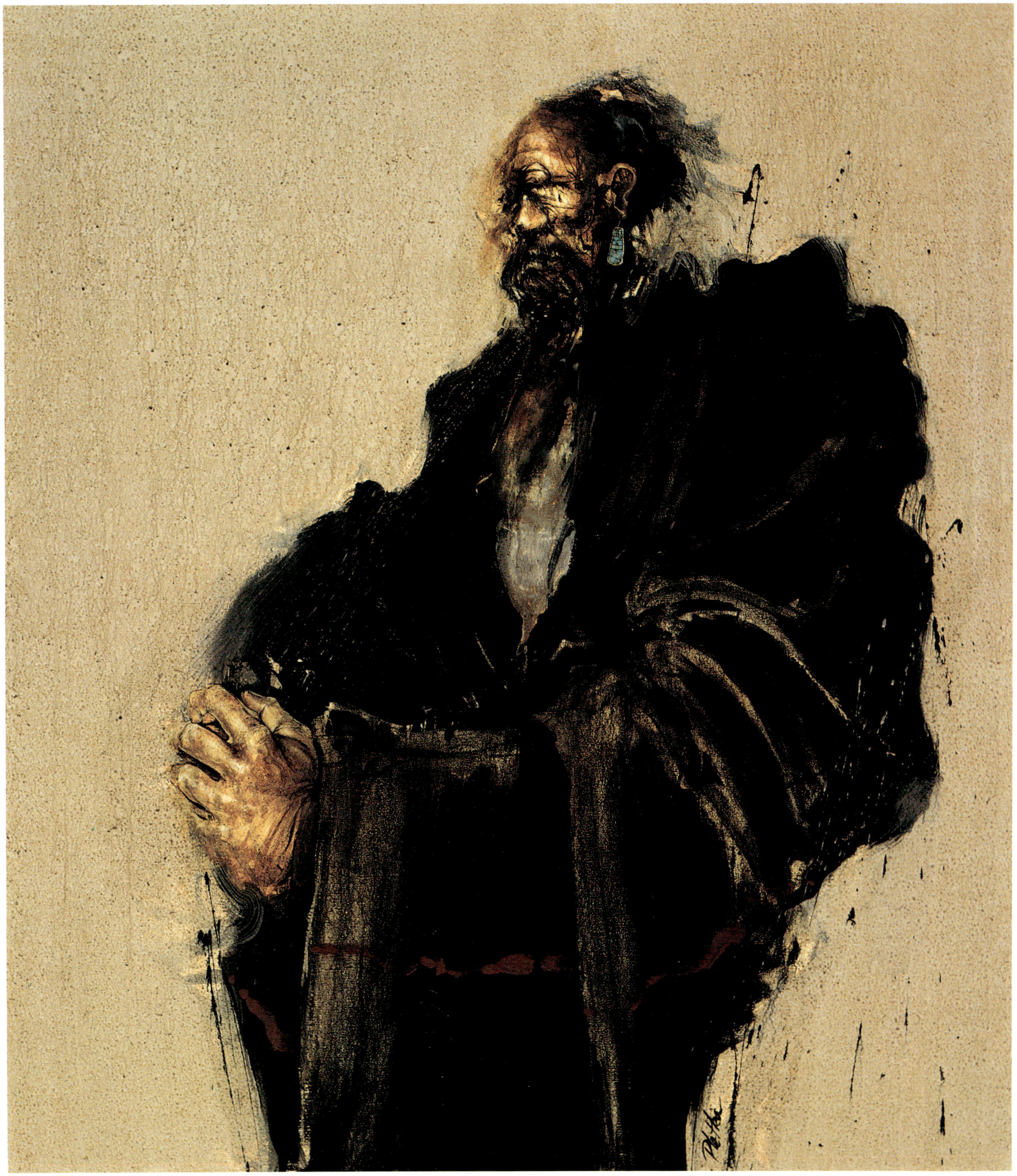

Hawikuh
1976
Acrylic on linen canvas
60 x 72

Completed in October 1976, *Hawikuh* depicts two Zuñi women who serve as pedestals for early examples of fine Zuñi pottery. The water jar at the left, executed between 1710 and 1770, is in the School of American Research collection in Santa Fe. Pletka discovered this Ashiwi polychrome jar in the book, *Historic Pottery of the Pueblo Indians,* by Larry Frank and Francis H. Harlow. The newer pot on the right belongs to anthropologist Richard Howard.

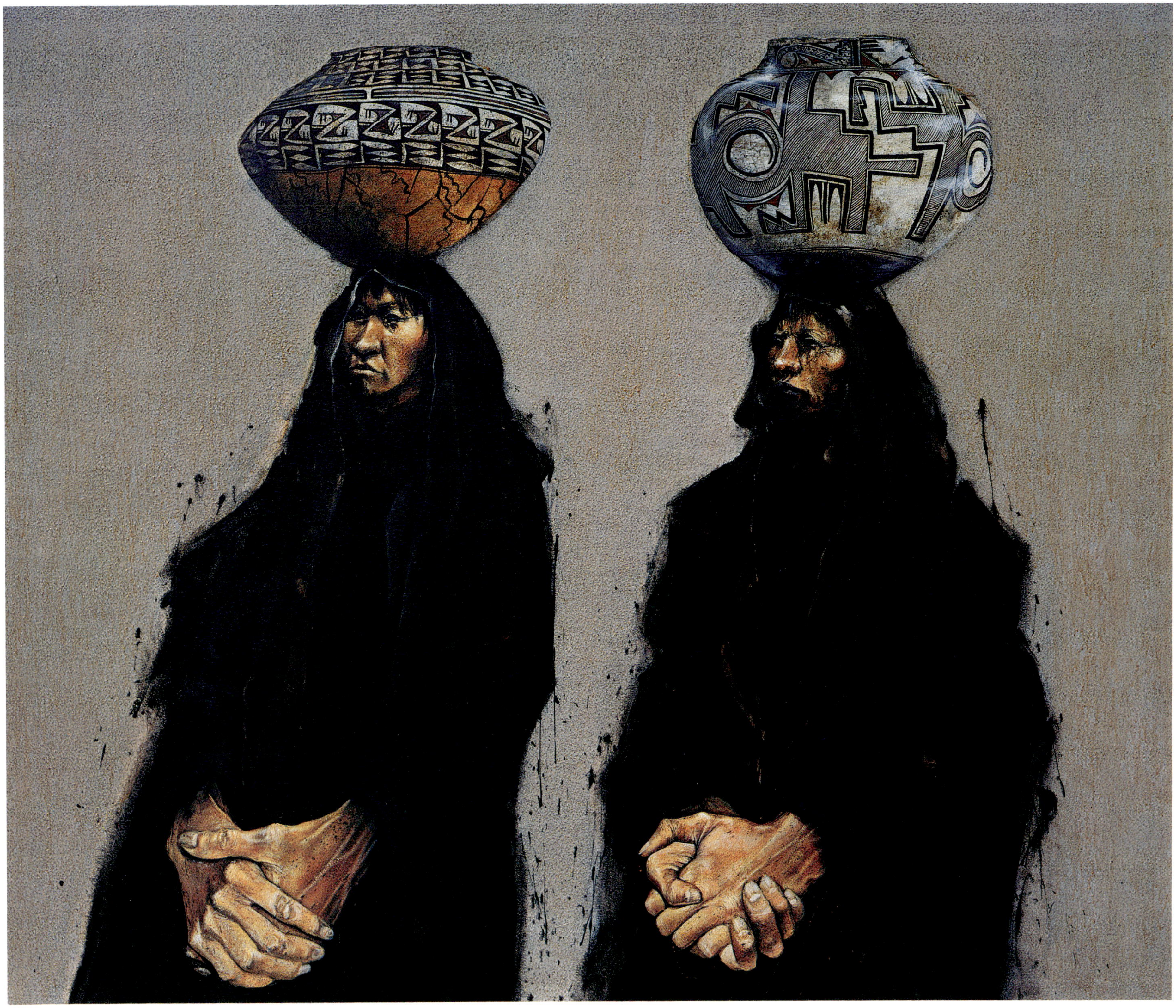

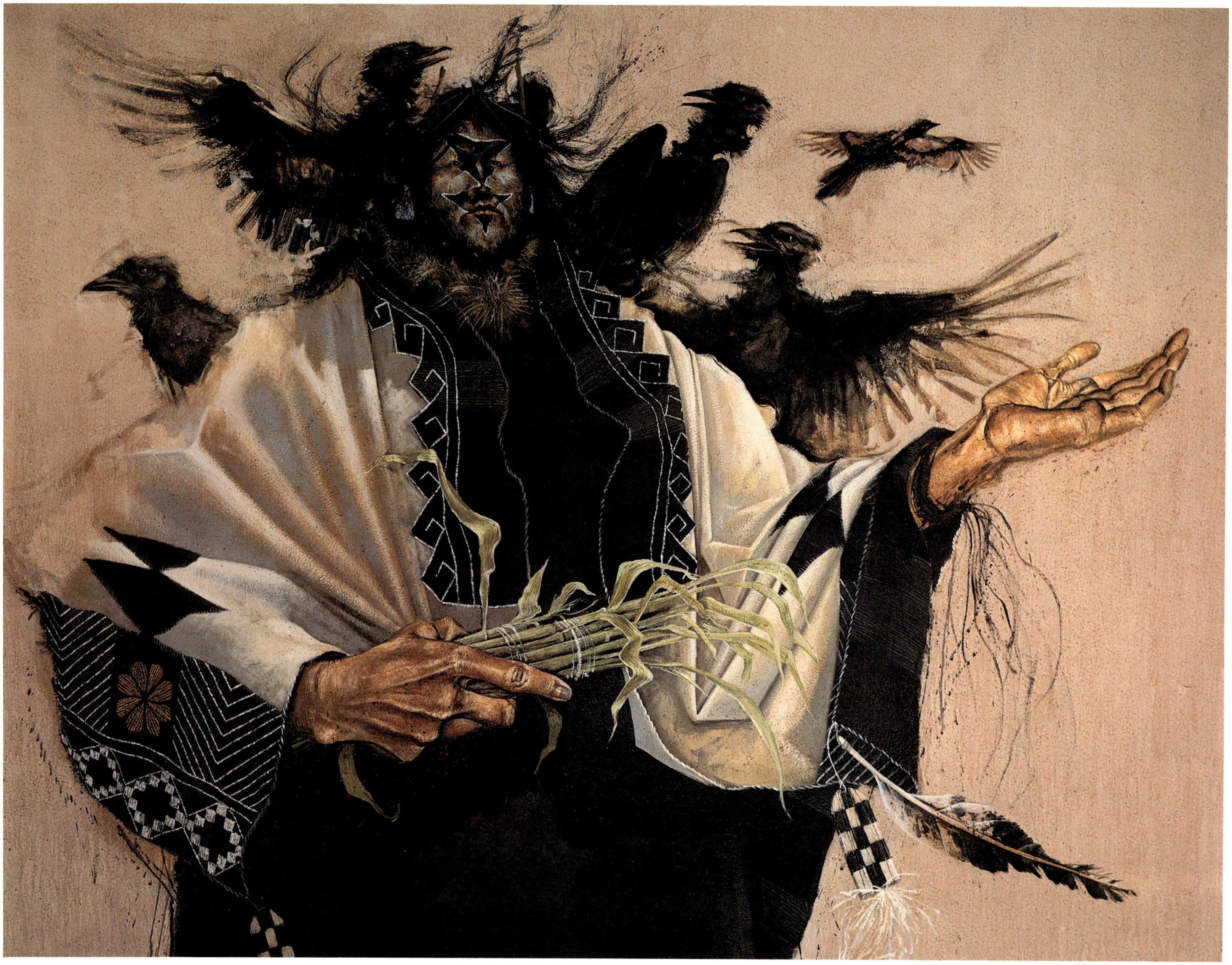

While The Ravens Laughed
1976
Acrylic on linen canvas
54 x 72

The Hopi Crow Bride kachina, or Angwushahai-i, is pictured in human form. Dolls and dancers representing the Crow Mother generally wear masks with ears of huge crow wings. Pletka brought the symbol to life.

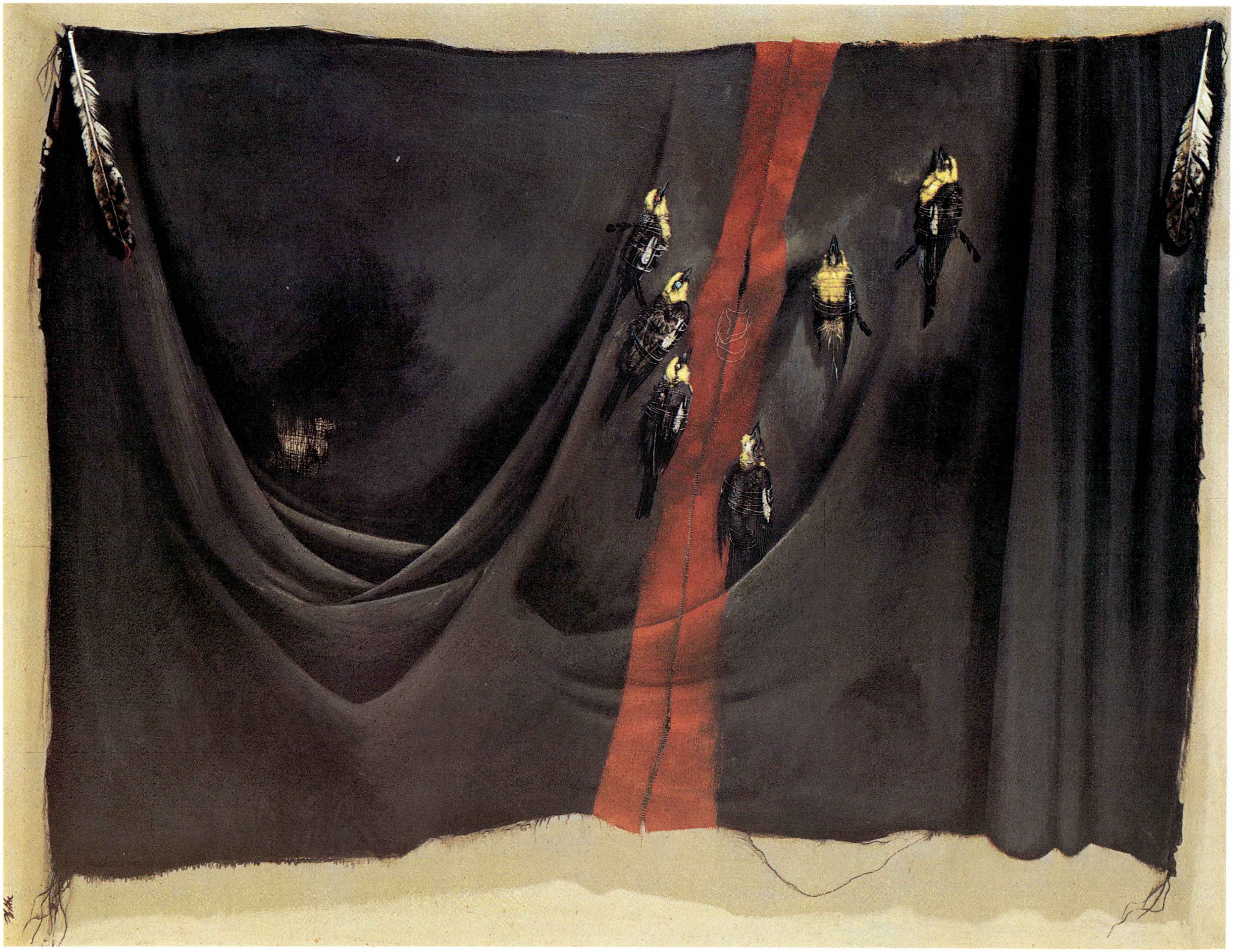

Strawberries for Tobacco
1976
Acrylic on linen canvas
54 x 72

Generally, Pletka showcases historical treasures by draping them over human forms. In this instance, the object is depicted in isolation of environment. This type of blanket was worn by members of the blackbird branch of the Strawberry Chapter of the Crow Tobacco Society.

Elk Song
1976
Acrylic on linen canvas
48 x 66

The Plains Indian elk dreamer wears a beaded war shirt with more than two hundred scalps appended to it. While levitating a hoop, he blows on an eagle bone whistle. His headdress includes the horns of a young bull elk. In Plains Indian belief, the elk was a symbol of sexuality and fertility. An elk dreamer was believed capable of influencing the actions and emotions of an intended lover by engaging in aphrodisiacal songs and ceremonies.

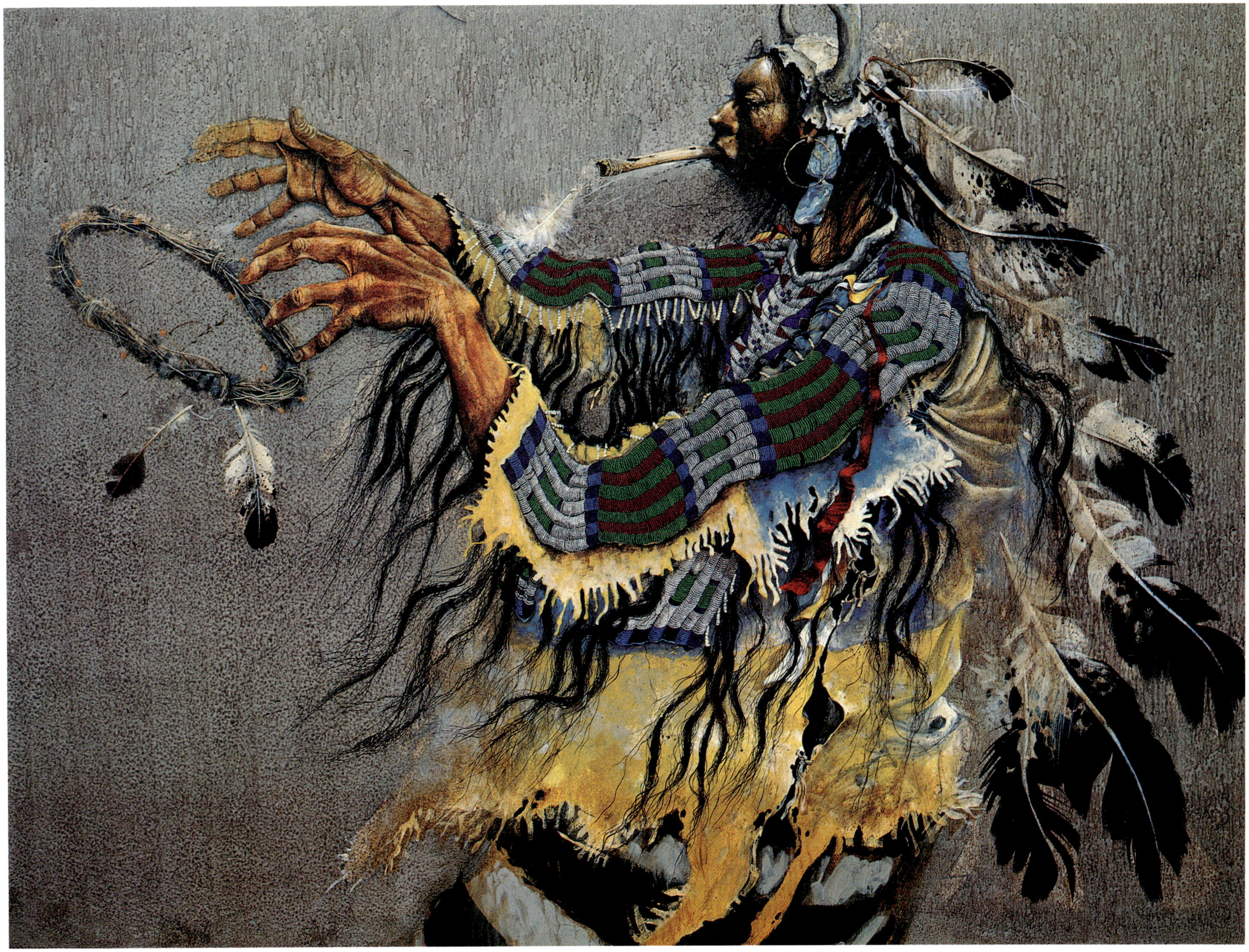

Hail Eagle
1976
Acrylic on linen canvas
30 x 48

Executed in only two days, *Hail Eagle* was the first work Pletka completed after moving to Arizona from Colorado. The predominating cool grays, applied in a watercolor approach, are shattered by the intense green of the Northern Plains warrior's atypically patterned face paint with hail spots. He wears a dead stuffed eagle to bolster his protective war medicine.

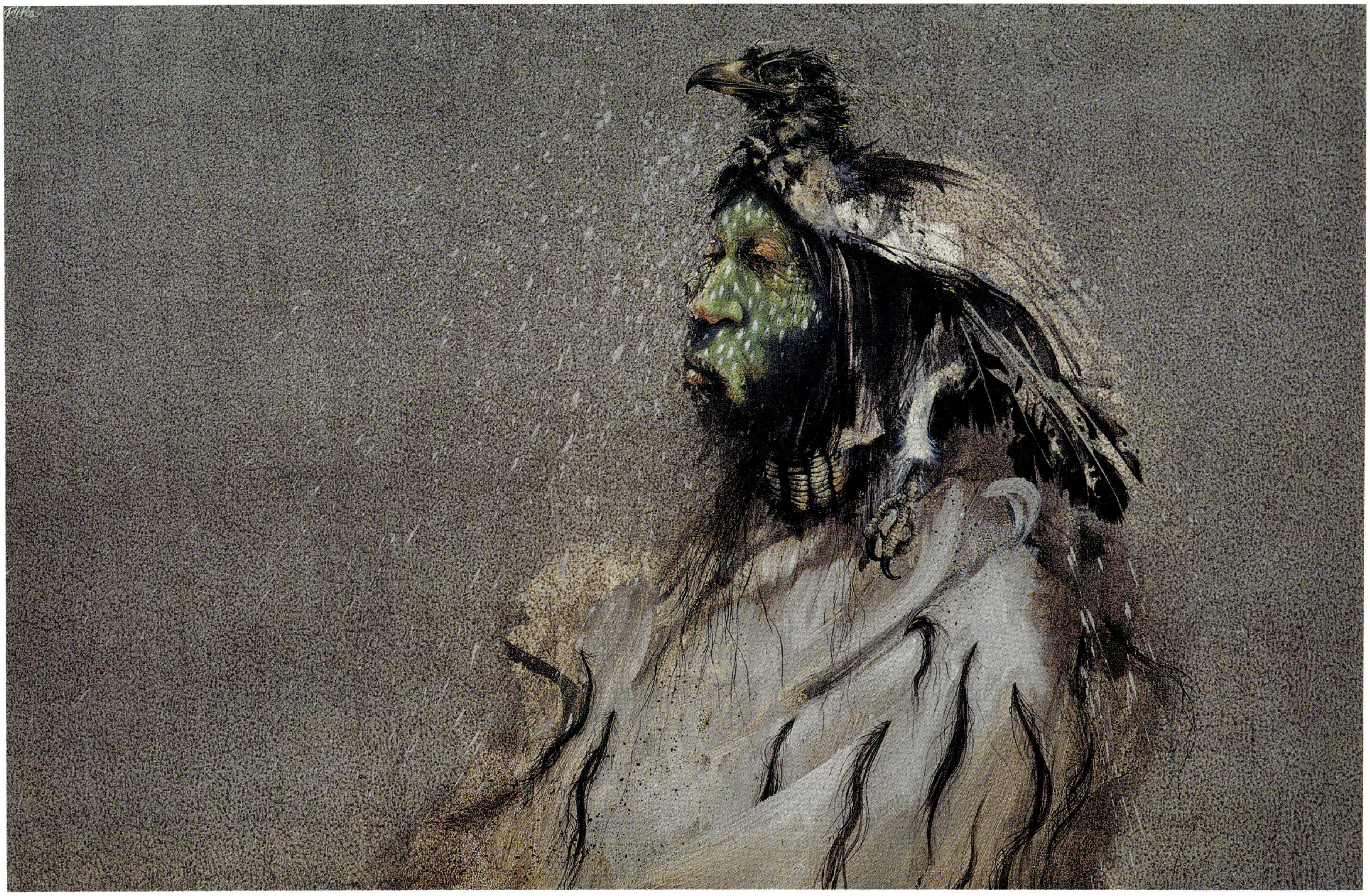

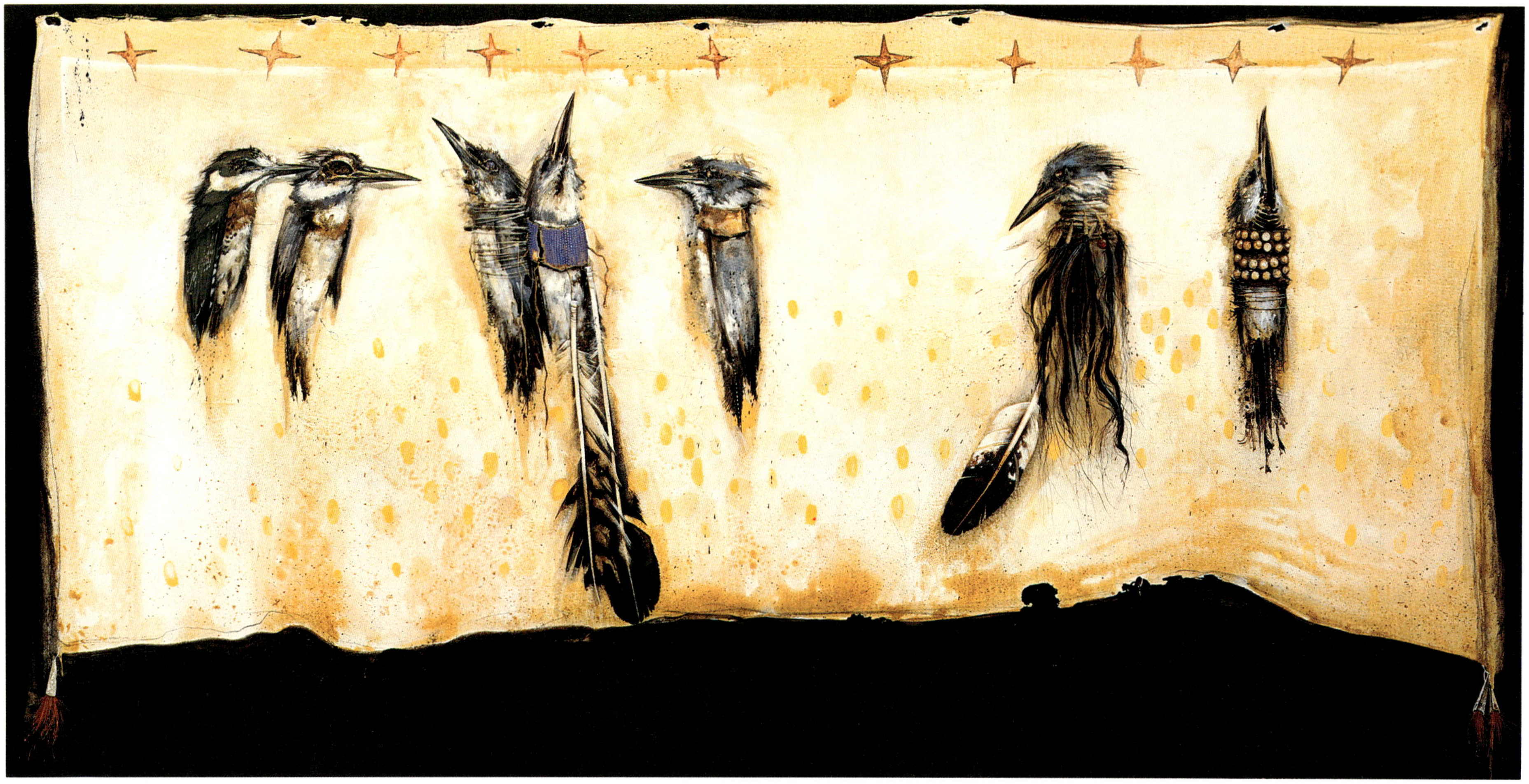

Eagle That Walks By the River No. II
1976
Acrylic on linen canvas
30 x 60

The title refers to Pletka's uncle, who at birth was named by Hopi neighbors. Translated, his name was Eagle-Who-Goes-Home-Walking. Some tribes believed kingfishers possessed the power to stop bullets or seal bullet or arrow wounds, because these birds dive into water without creating rings or ripples. It was believed the wearer of a dead kingfisher would be imbued with an ability to become impervious to bullet wounds. The green kingfisher is from the Rio Grande Valley. The others are a series of male and female belted kingfishers. The yellow spots on the buckskin are hail spots. Yellow was a sacred color among the Cheyenne, as well as some other Plains tribes. Hail spots were said to conjure weather fronts or similar partitions between the wearer and the enemy.

Oh Holy Raven
1976
Acrylic on linen canvas
72 x 60

The Blackfoot Raven Society, one of numerous warrior fellowships, was reserved exclusively for old men. It was founded by a Blackfoot Indian who dreamed of a crow that metamorphosed into a man and gave orders to inaugurate the Raven Society. The crow prescribed clothing, ornaments, and painted symbols, all of which would serve as power sources for the members. The headdress in the painting is patterned after existing examples. Only two members of the society were permitted to wear it. Traditionally, the forehead was painted red, the sacred color, mottled with white spots, representing bird excrement. Here, Pletka has added body paint to the forearm and abdomen. The painting illustrates the Blackfoot's immersion in animism by dramatizing a reverse transformation—from man to crow.

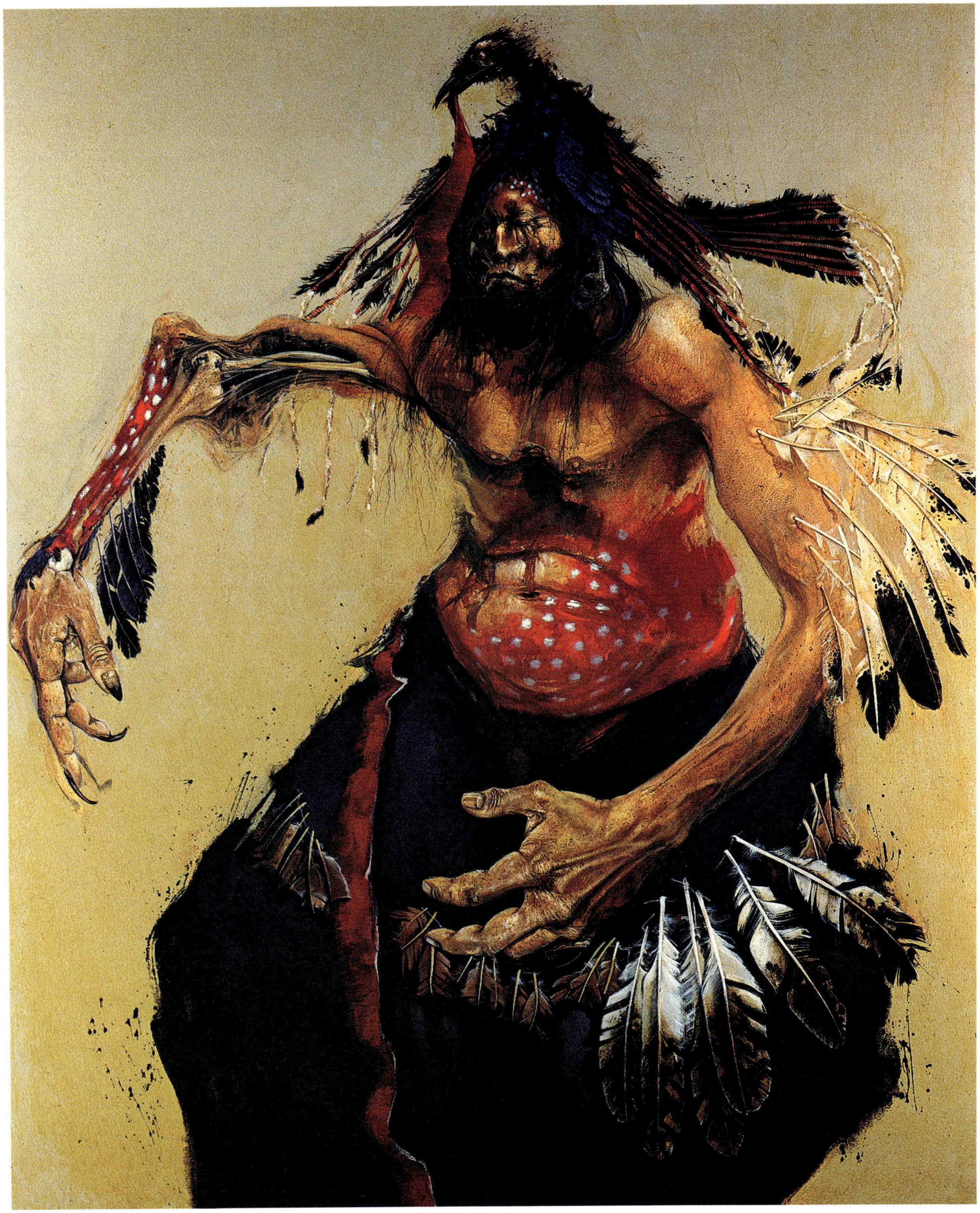

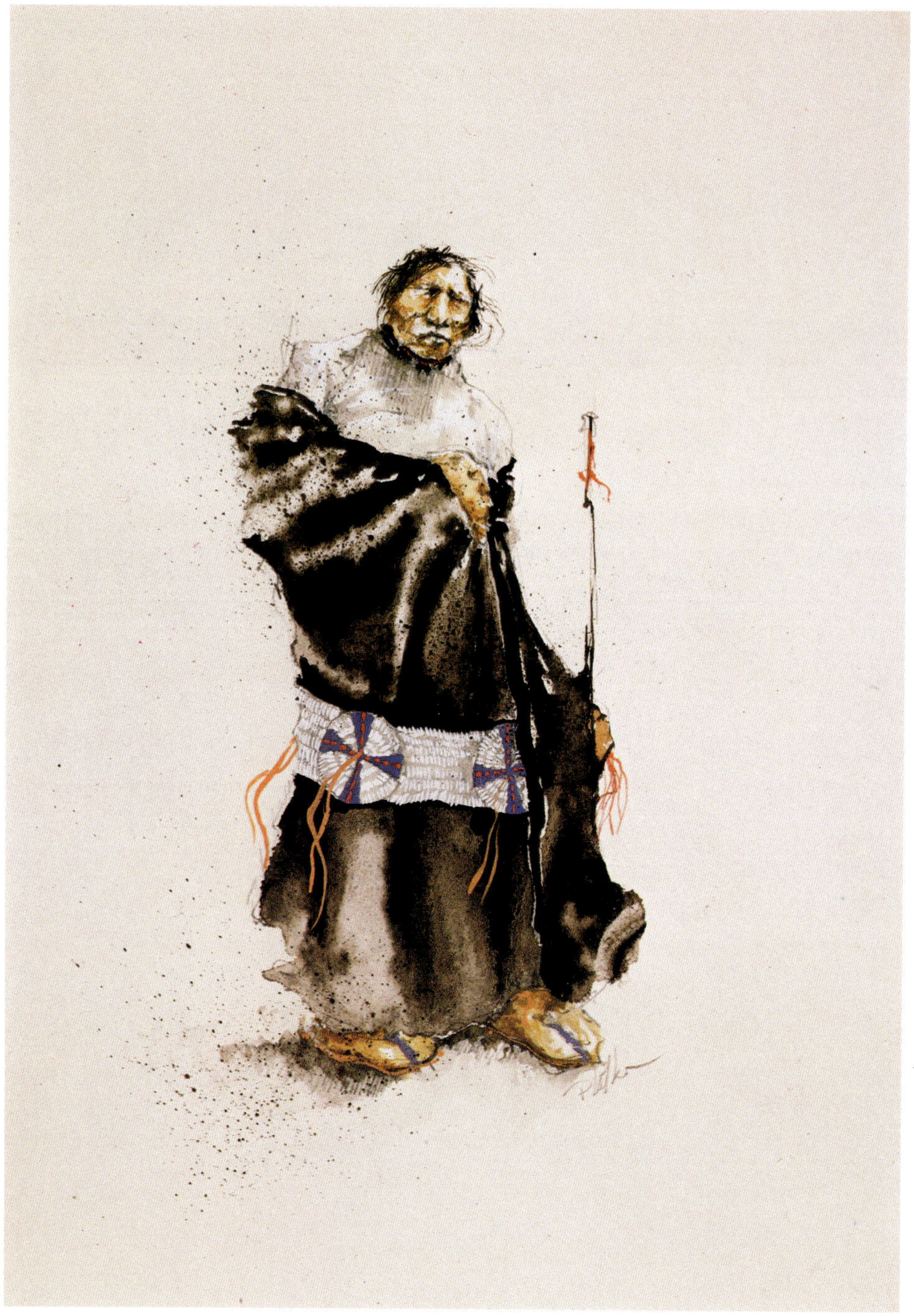

Uintah
1976
Watercolor
7 x 5

Uintah is the name of a band of Ute Indians. The rather plain clothing is significant of reservation dress in the late 1800s. Most western Plains Indians wore trousers, simple moccasins, and a shirt. They completed their outfit by wrapping in a blanket.

War Bonnet
1976
Watercolor
5 x 7

Pletka painted this little study of a bonnet as a preliminary for a larger piece. Although he has tried several times, it has never worked in another scale. A military headdress, it is depicted with brass shoe buttons across the brow band; its base is red stroud.

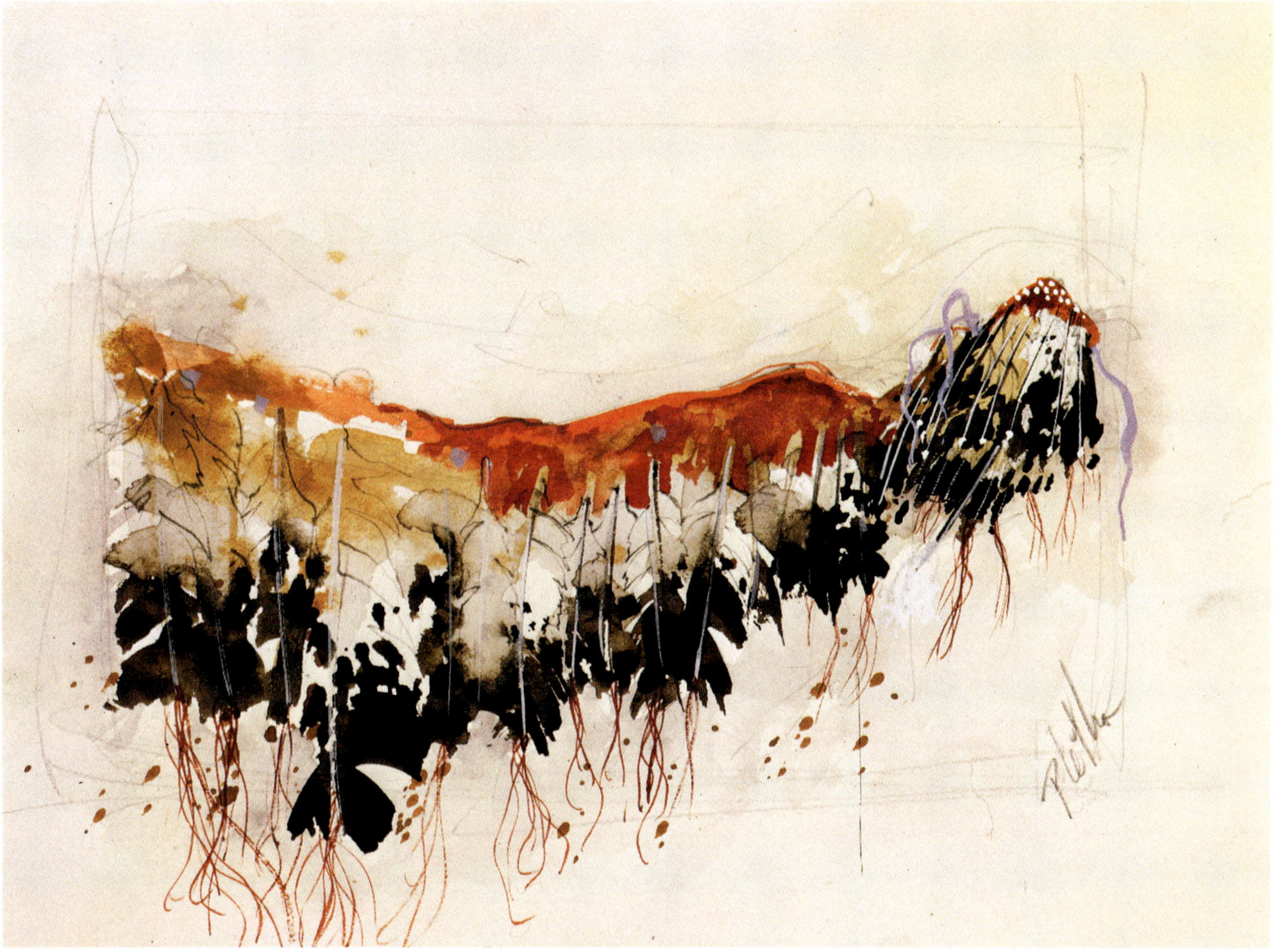

Kills Night
1977
Acrylic on linen canvas
42 x 54

The Blackfoot's hair is knotted at the crown, a style preferred among early tribes along the Missouri River. He wears a raven with ribbons streaming from its tail and brass hawk bells tied to its feet.

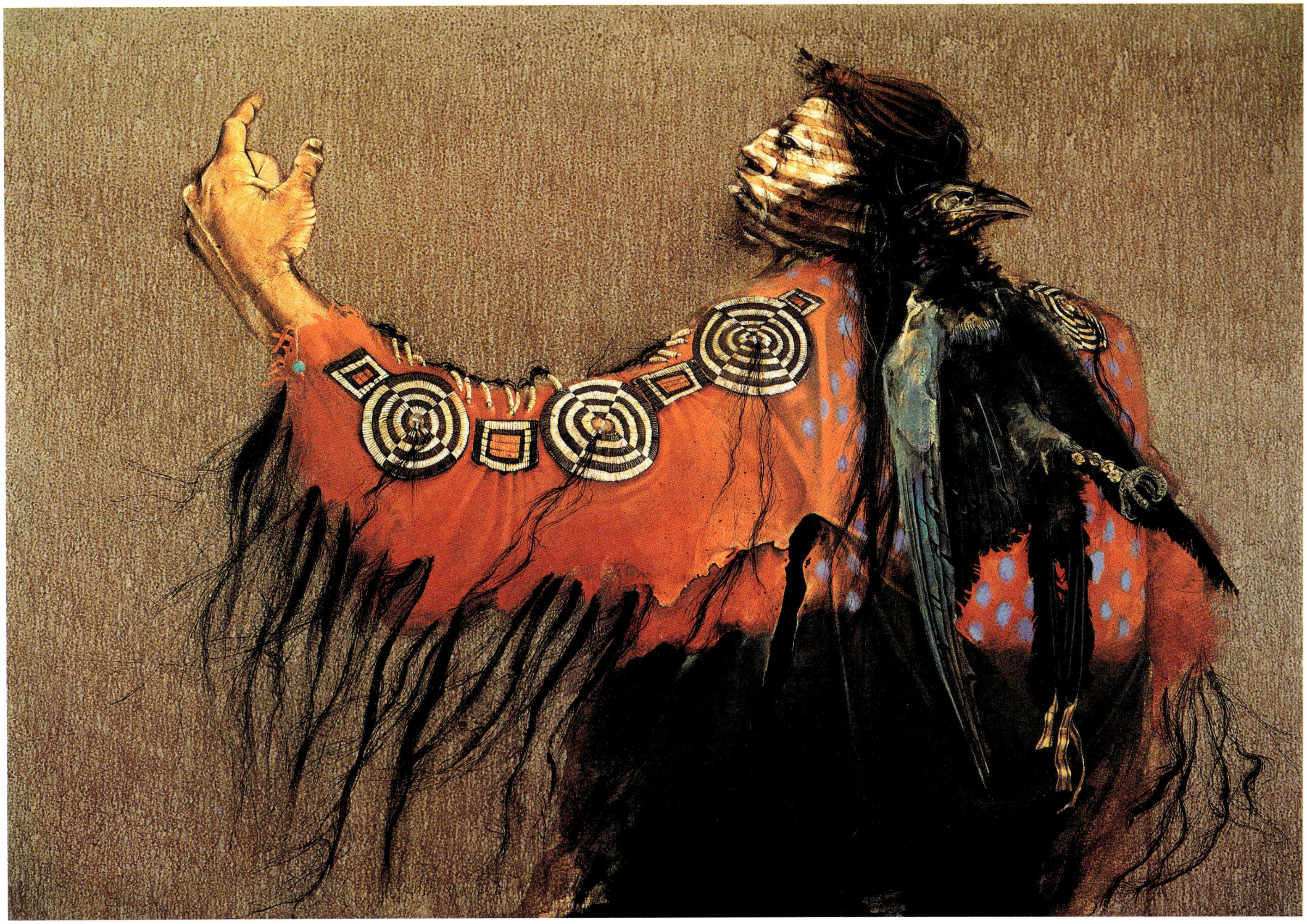

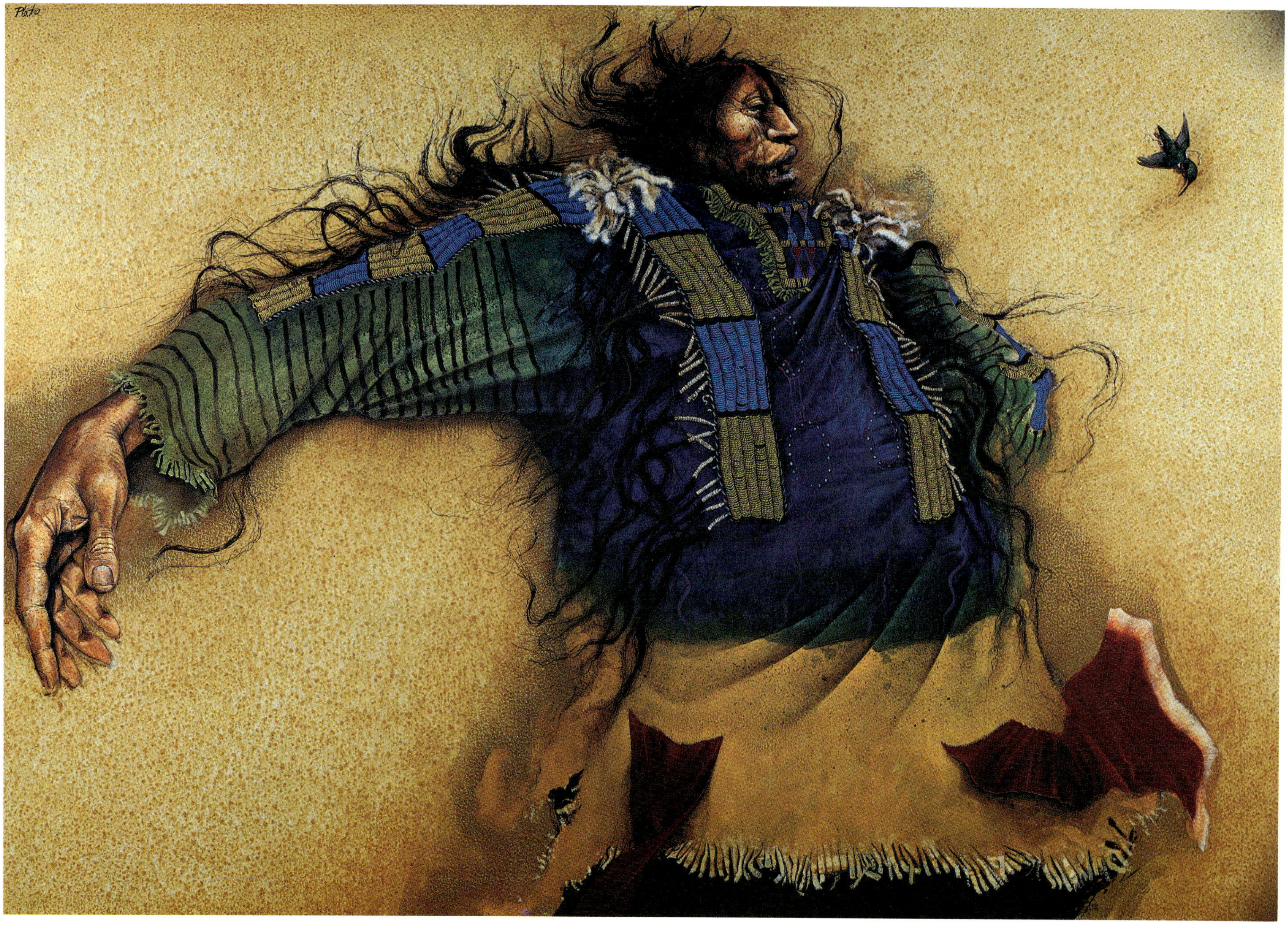

Nothing Lives Forever But the Rock
1977
Acrylic on linen canvas
40 x 58

"Nothing lives forever but the rock" is a line from a famous Cheyenne war song chanted by White Antelope as he was killed during the battle at Sand Creek. The painting captures the death of a Cheyenne warrior and may be viewed from two perspectives: as an upright man against an abstract background or as a supine body casting shadows against the sand. At right lies a frozen hummingbird. The shirt, collected by the Chicago Historical Society in the early 1900s and now privately owned, is a typical 1850s to 1860s Cheyenne war shirt with scalp locks from either relatives or fallen enemies and a bib with ermine clusters at the shoulders. The stripes on the sleeves may have indicated significant events in the warrior's career.

Sun Dance
1978
Acrylic on linen canvas
40 x 58

The Sun Dance was a rite of spring designed to celebrate the gifts of the sun and cleanse the body of impurities. Participants demonstrated their supreme devotion by sacrificing pieces of flesh or engaging in acts of self-torture. This painting, based in part on George Catlin's *Mandan Torture Ceremony,* drawn about 1832, highlights participants from an Upper Missouri River tribe—Hidatsa, Blackfoot, or Assiniboin. The Sun Dance heralded the northward return of buffalo herds. During this time of year, puberty ceremonies were conducted and ears were pierced. In the ritual pictured, the flesh of the chest is skewered and pulled taut by ropes wrapped around a sacred center pole or tree. The men are suspended or dancing, constantly tugging against the line, until the jagged hooks cut through the flesh, freeing them. Dismissed as barbaric by missionaries and government authorities, the Sun Dance was viewed by Indians as a glorious renewal of sacred vows.

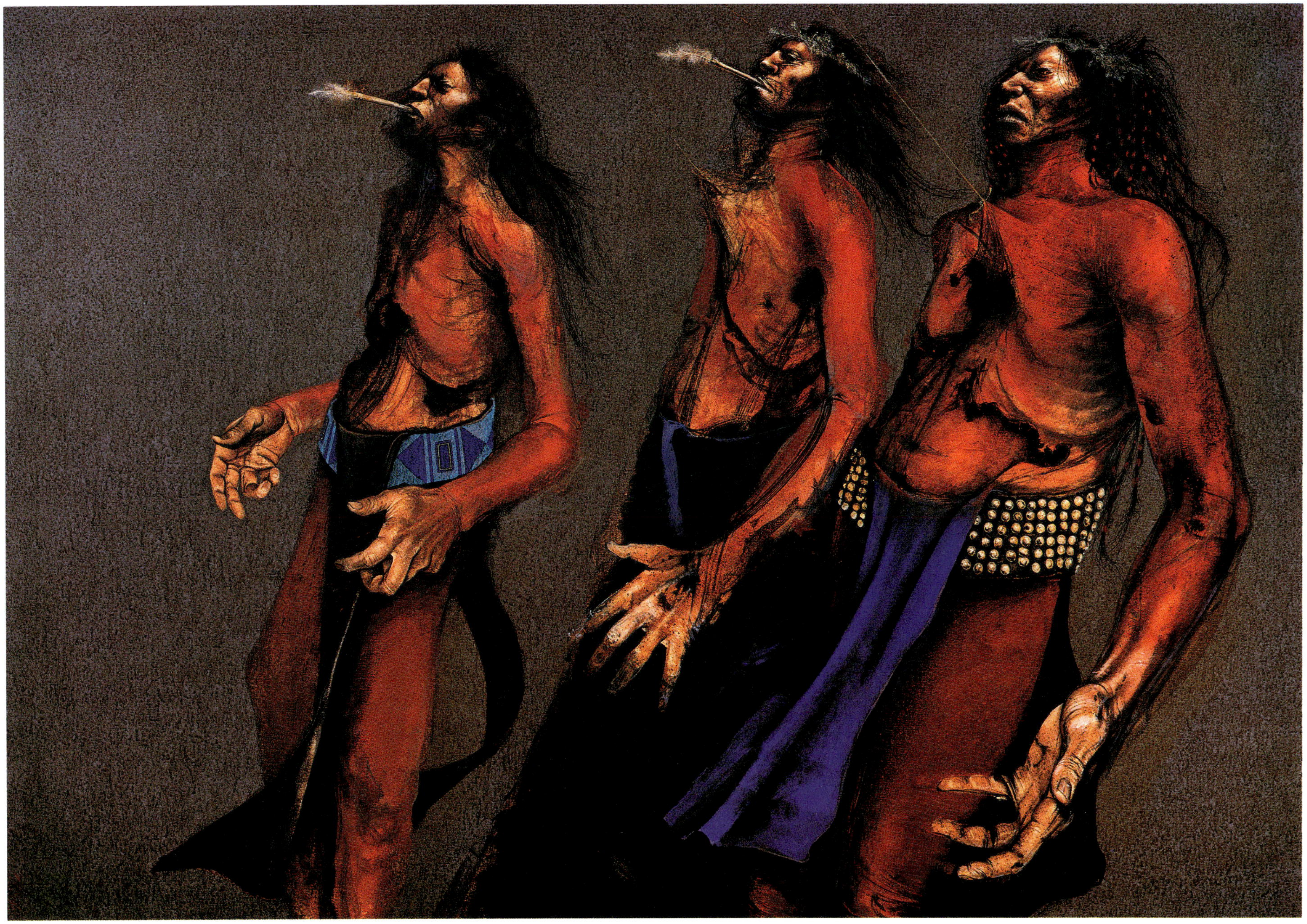

Wazhaze
1978
Acrylic on linen canvas
44 x 50

The Osage Indian wears what traditionally has been termed a wedding coat, but actually was patterned after a soldier coat and handmade of trade cloth. The garment typically was bedizened with colorful silk patches, brocade, satin ribbons, buttons, and beads. Pletka's invention includes a beaded hand, a favorite Osage design. Later Osage fashion would have incorporated a tall hat with an ostrich plume. Wazhaze wears an array of ear dangles, customary among the early prairie people, as indicated in illustrations by George Catlin and Karl Bodmer.

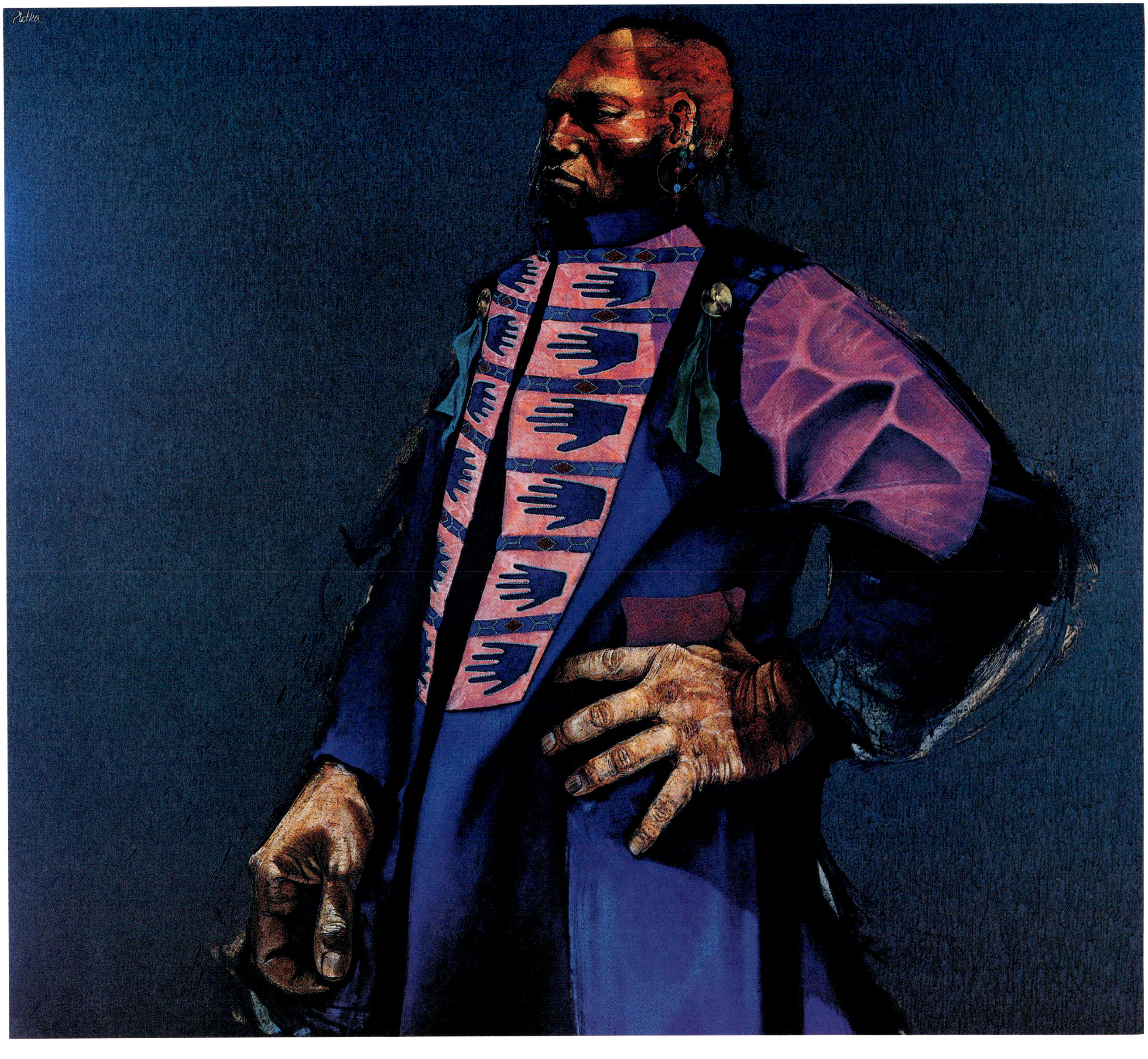
Pletka

Takes Back Twice
1978
Acrylic on linen canvas
50 x 62

Among the Crow and certain other northern tribes, skulls were saved from the scaffold burials of dead relatives. If during his lifetime the person had shown signs of being clairvoyant, then that attribute was presumed still active after death. The skull would be placed in a bundle and consulted from time to time on important matters—if something was lost or the individual wanted to know the potential success of a horse raid. The bundle would be opened, and offerings would be placed beside it. Sometimes, it would be painted and beads or colored feathers would be tied to it. "Takes Back Twice" is the name of a man whose skull is in an existing bundle.

The Crows are also very famous for their lovely medicine shields. This one is based on the shield owned by Rotten Belly. A heron was appended to the original shield, but in this instance, Pletka has used the head and neck of a whooping crane. Tied to it is an umbilical charm, a quilled leather imitation of a sand lizard, containing the umbilical cord of the shield's owner. The blue figure on the shield is a water monster, a mythological being.

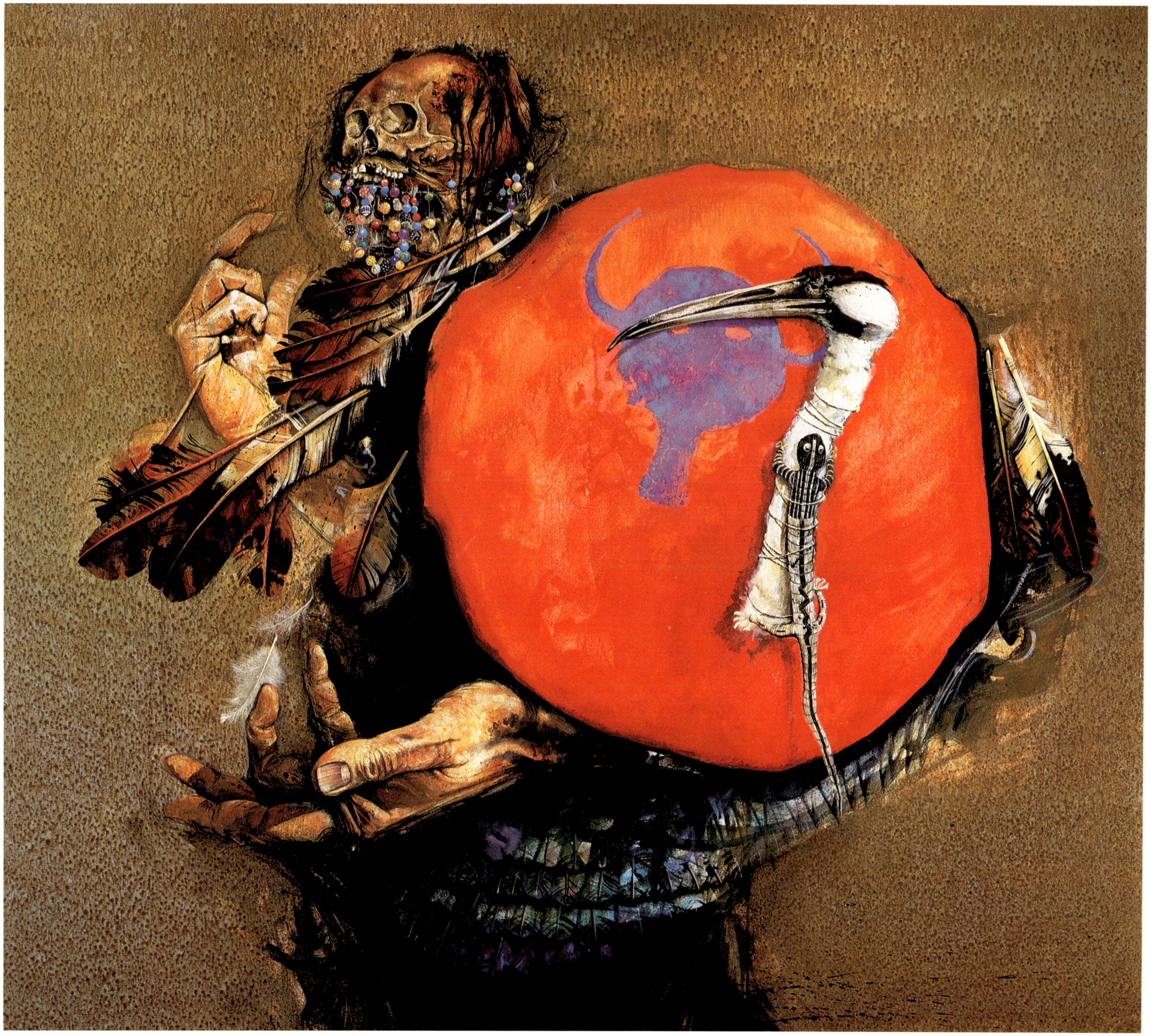

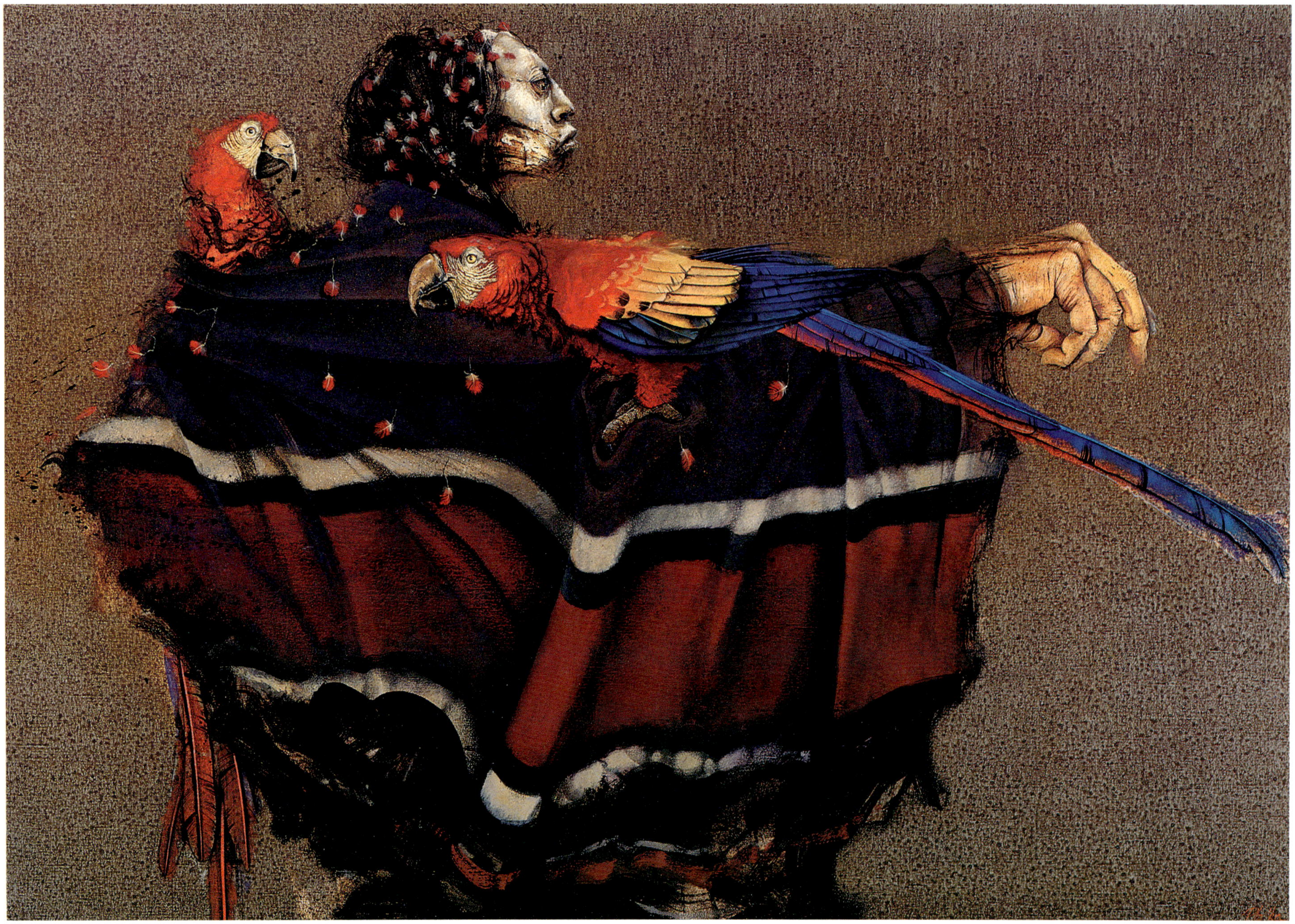

Cacique
1978
Acrylic on linen canvas
40 x 58

Pueblo Indians occasionally traded with southern people to obtain exotic birds, especially parrots, from Mexico and farther south. This Taos man, daubed with white paint, wears a Rio Grande blanket and serves as a perch for two South American macaws. Because parrots are considered sacred among Pueblo people, a renowned Santa Clara potter refused to gaze at the painting, which she found disquieting and incisive.

Leroy
1978
Acrylic on linen canvas
48 x 60

Leroy is one of few Pletka paintings dealing with contemporary subjects. Pletka was struck one day by an Indian man strolling in downtown Santa Fe. The figure seemed a living example of a fierce Cheyenne or Kiowa warrior of the 1870s. Taken by his facial features, Pletka persuaded the man, Leroy, to pose for the portrait. The Southern Cheyenne shirt Leroy wears was once owned by Pletka. In the background, a tepee liner bears a warrior drawing of a man stealing horses, considered an honorable profession among Plains Indians.

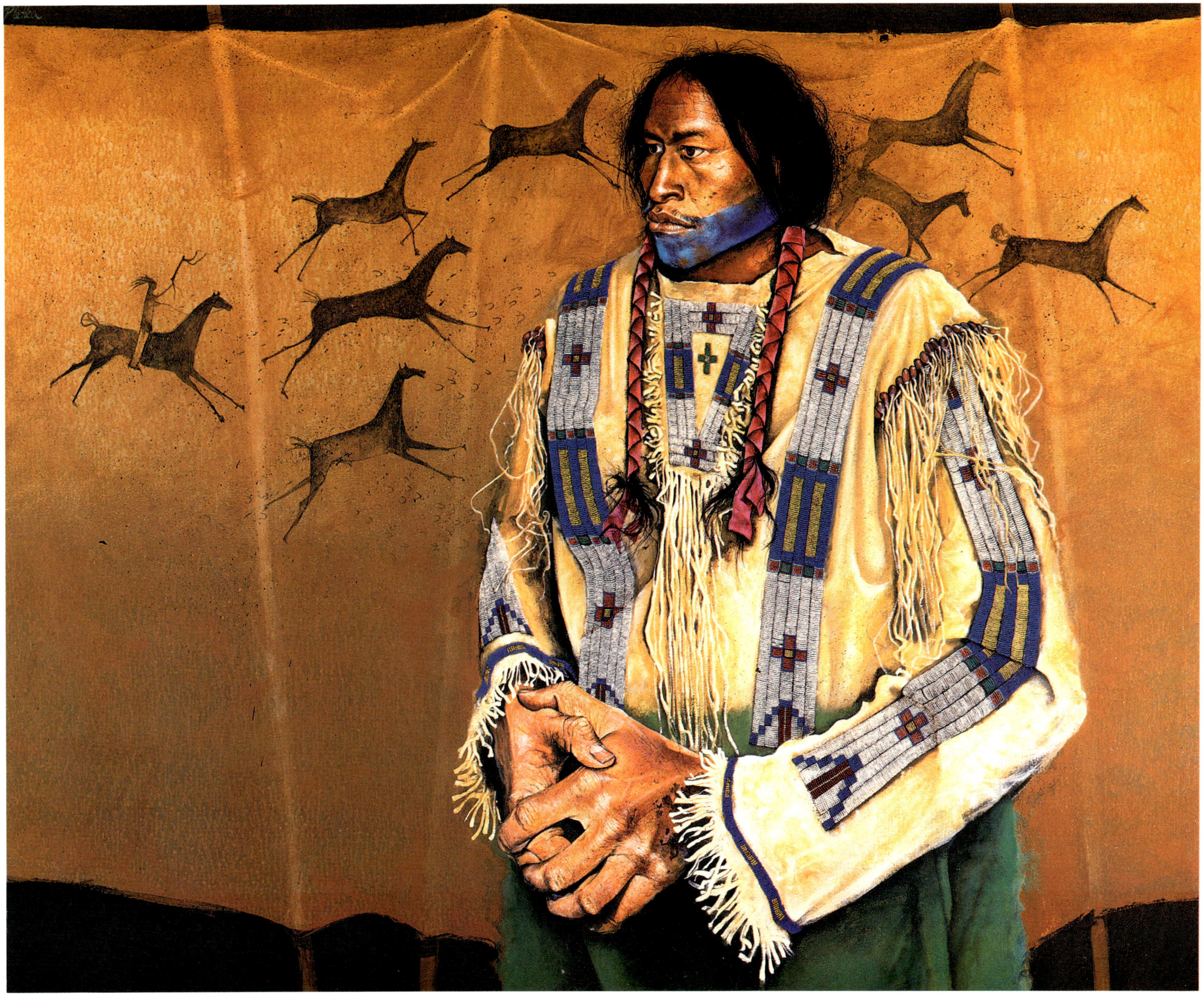

One Who Does Not Give Away
1978
Acrylic on linen canvas
30 x 40

This portrait hints at the parallels among aboriginal cultures worldwide. Though the figure bears the posture and accoutrements of an American Indian, his features could be of any tribal origin. The painting portrays a northern man of the Upper Missouri River in the late 1700s, when Lewis and Clark might have seen him. He is smeared with blue paint, probably a mixture of indigo and clay, striped with yellow earth. He wears a beaded collar, not unlike many worn by African tribes today. The collar is a forerunner of a hair pipe choker that became extremely popular in the 1800s. He also flaunts a ring in his nose, another popular ornament of the period and a costume trait that prompted French trappers to name an Idaho tribe the Nez Perce, or "pierced nose."

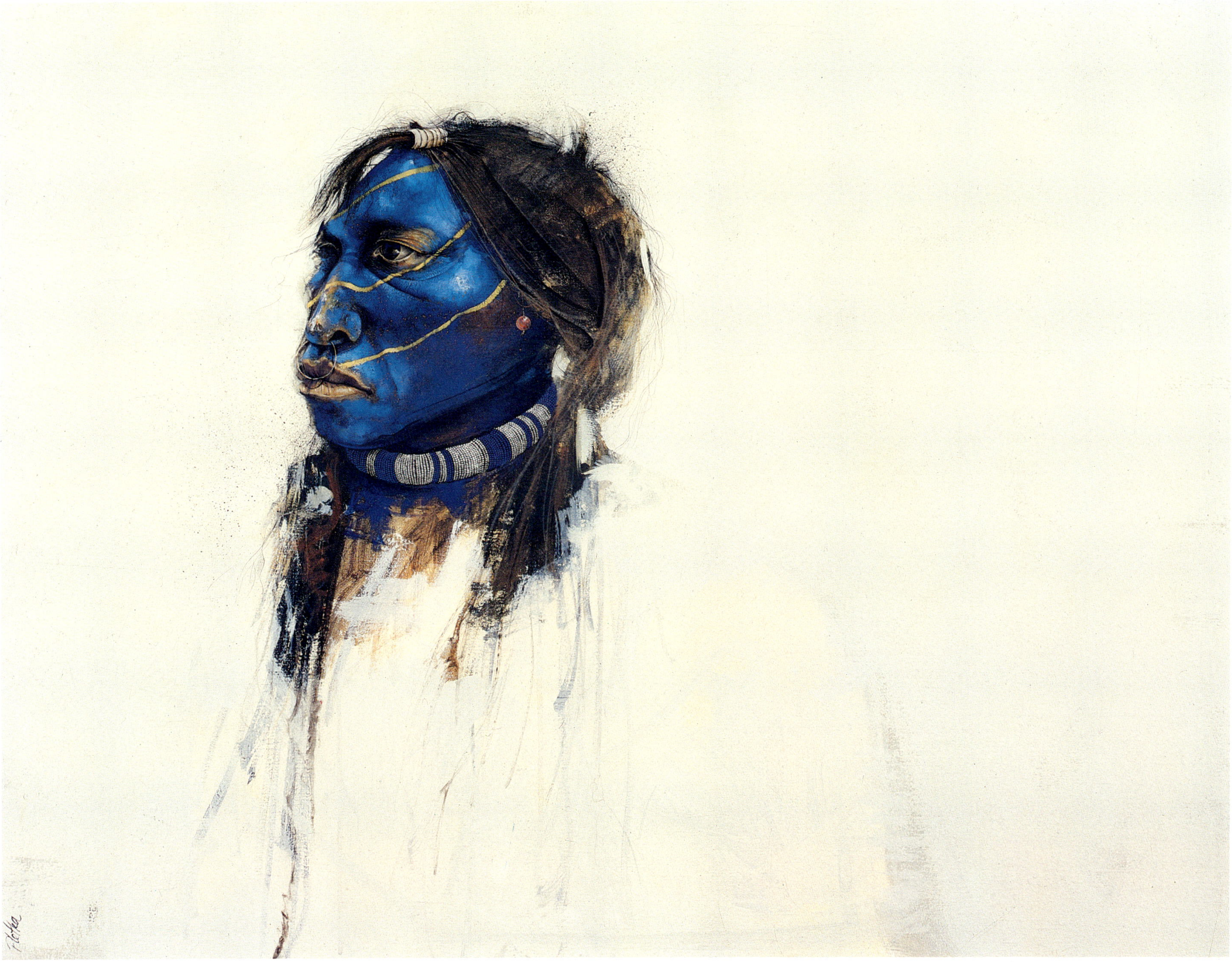

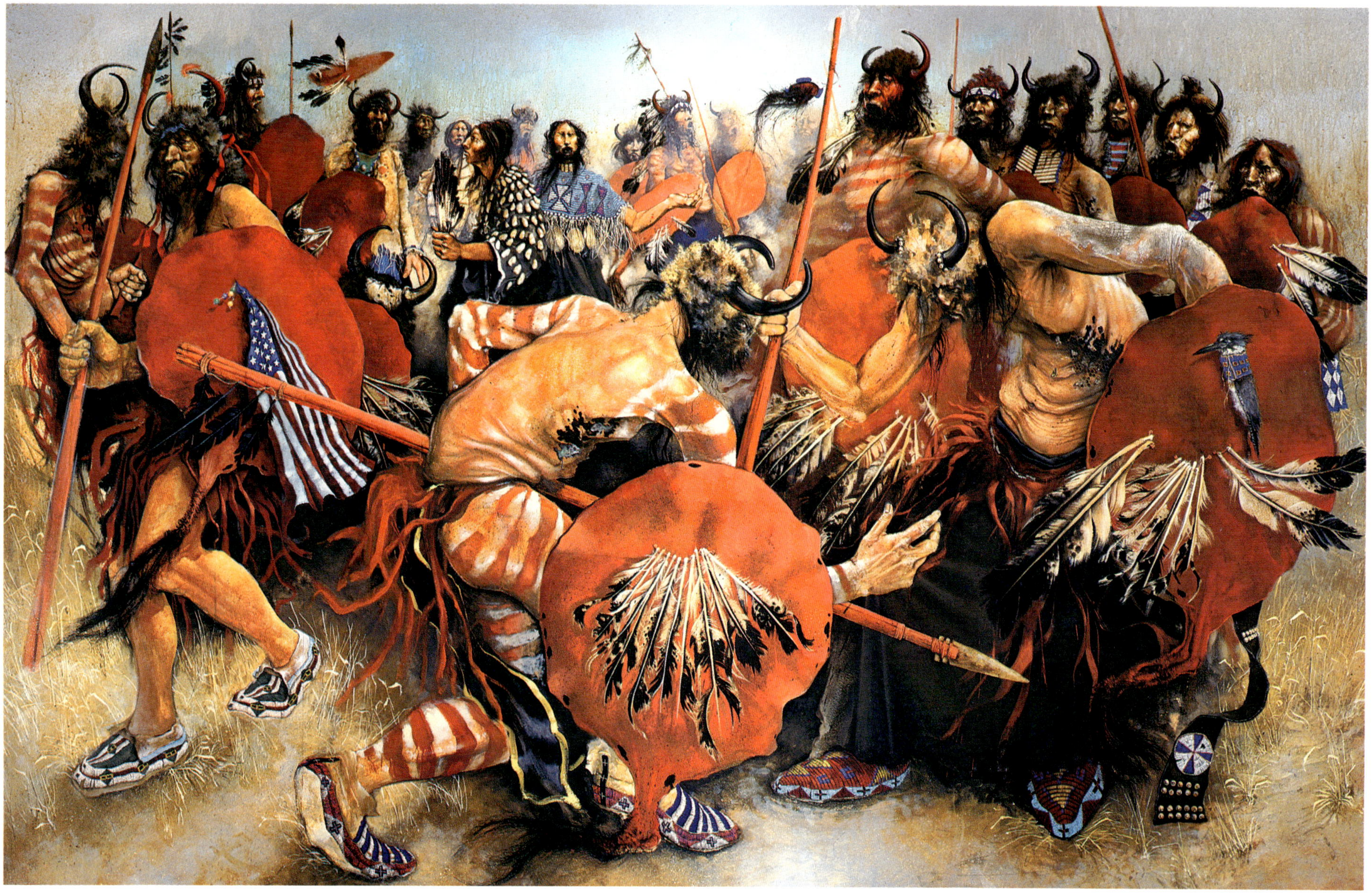

Red Talkers
1978
Acrylic on linen canvas
72 x 120

Red Talkers, the Indian name for Cheyenne, are pictured here engaged in the Bull Society Dance. This military society consisted mainly of the tribe's older soldiers. During the dance, members imitate old bull buffaloes by snorting, grunting, pawing the ground, and charging. Prescribed shields, made from the buffalo's hindquarters, with the tail still attached and painted red, were brandished. Often, feathers, fetishes, or a dancer's personal medicine were tied to the shield as well. Horned headdresses were worn, and the men danced feverishly in a circle around four chaste girls considered sacred and selected by the society to symbolize fertility. Three are shown here; one wears an elk tooth dress and carries a feather fan. As the dance becomes more turbulent, the men feel themselves being transformed into bull buffaloes. Pletka's painting unveils the desired metamorphosis. The riveting figure in the foreground is assuming the appearance of the buffalo. Metaphorically, his personal medicine symbols, green mice, are emerging from his rib cage as his power asserts itself. The opposing dancer similarly feels his medicine take life, as his flesh parts to reveal bees and honeycomb.

Star Lookers
1978
Acrylic on linen canvas
48 x 60

With this painting, Pletka began to treat figures less as mountainous weights and more as sculptures, pleasingly arranged in a three-dimensional environment. Ceremonial lances have been stabbed in the ground where three Pawnees meet to converse about sacred matters. The figure at the left wears a first phase Navajo chief blanket and prairie style moccasins. The man in the background wears a military coat, cherished by Pawnees. On the right, the figure wears a buffalo robe depicting a buffalo hunt and a headdress patterned after a similar one-horned version owned by Petalesharp, a Skidi Pawnee chief credited for preventing a captive girl from being put to death during a Pawnee Morning Star ceremony.

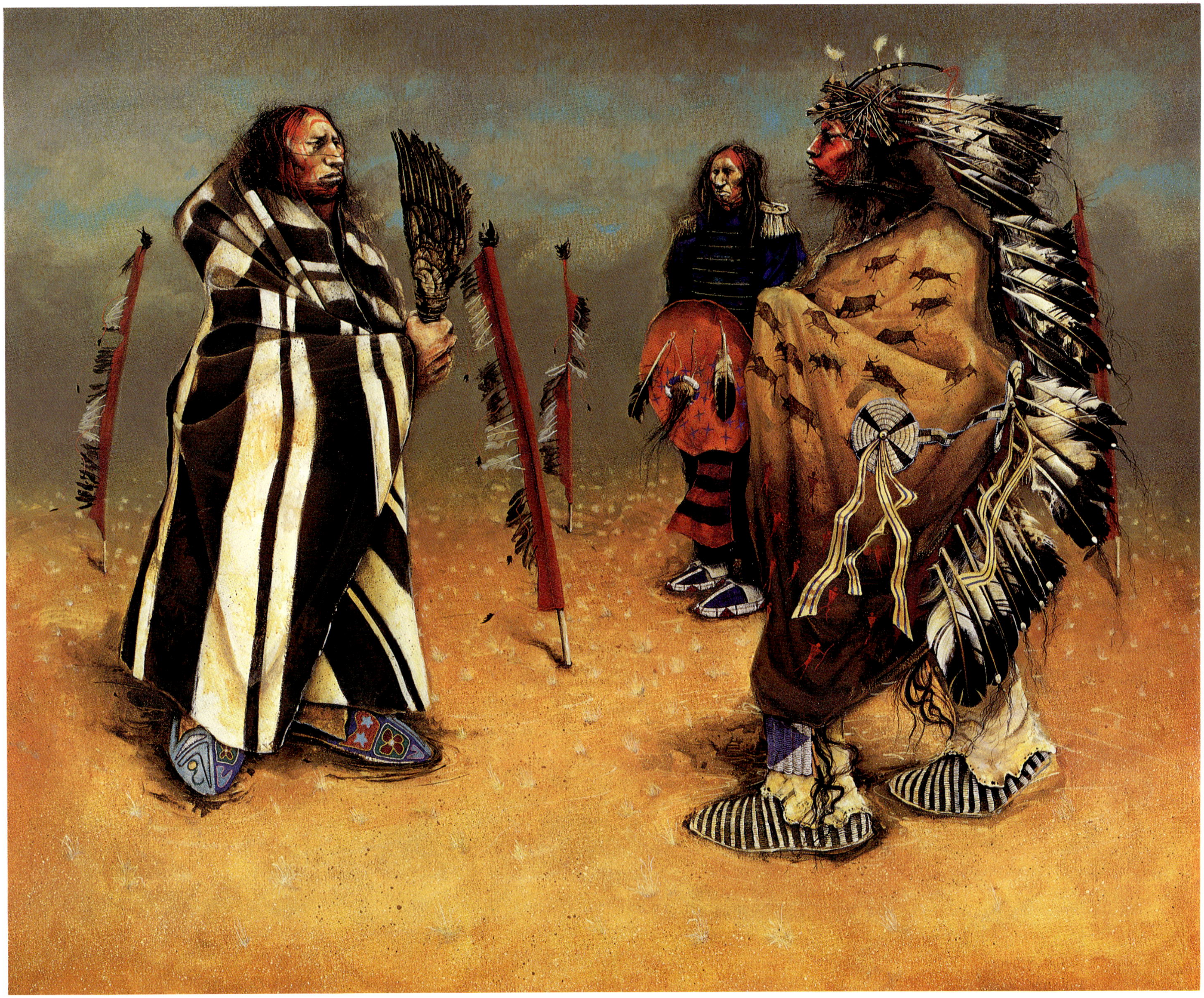

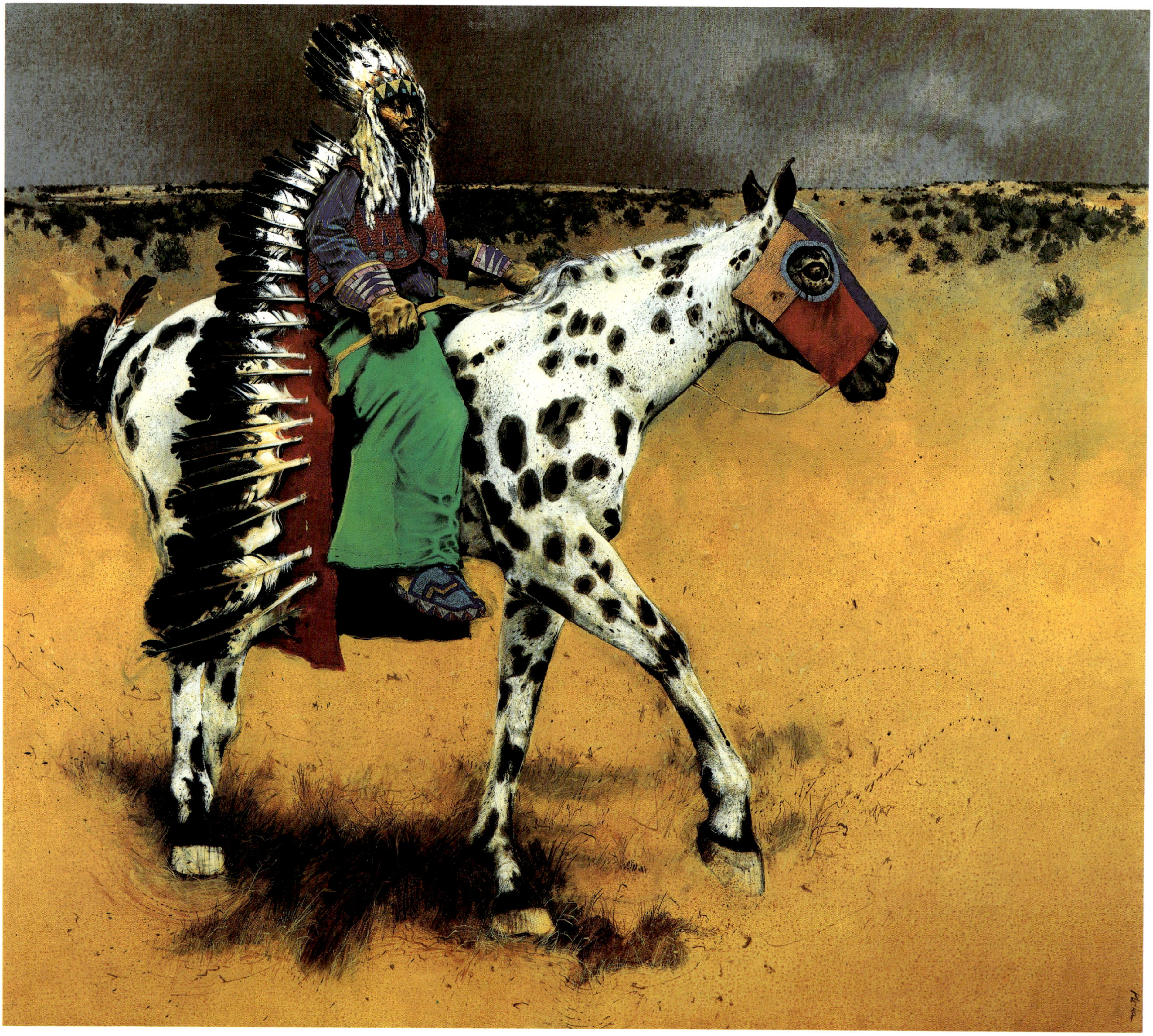

Pend d'Oreille
1979
Acrylic on linen canvas
52 x 60

The Kalispel Indians of the Northern Plateau—named Pend d'Oreille (ear drop) by French traders because of their large shell earrings—borrowed much of their dress and mannerisms from the Blackfoot and similar tribes. Interestingly, the Pend d'Oreille Indians, like the Palouse and Nez Perce, developed the Appaloosa, a rugged saddle horse with a mottled coat. The Pend d'Oreille rides an Appaloosa stallion with a horse mask typical among Northern Plateau tribes. The animal's tail is tied in preparation for war. The rider wears green blanket leggings, an erect Nez Perce headdress, a red beaded vest, and gauntlets. The painting exhibits Pletka's move from dominating, pyramidal figures toward fuller landscapes and stronger foreground.

Talks to Gods
1979
Acrylic on linen canvas
52 x 60

A transitional piece, *Talks to Gods* comments on the parallels and differences between Indian sacred culture and Christianity. The Franciscan priest wears a Chinese silk brocade chasuble found in Puebla, Mexico. The stole with the skull vignette is Pletka's invention, though the idea was borrowed from El Greco's *The Burial of Count Orgaz*. The father, a representative of the Christian Trinity, speaks with Sholawitsi, a Zuñi fire god and delegate of the Sun, one of three deities. During the winter Shalako ceremony at Zuñi Pueblo, Sholawitsi and Sayatasha, the northern rain god, plant prayer sticks and smoke native tobacco in a ritual designed to bring rain. Sholawitsi prepares the way for the Shalakos, ten-foot couriers of the rainmakers, whose impersonators carry their masks on poles. The birdlike Shalakos bless the houses of the townspeople.

Pletka considers *Talks to Gods* a milestone, a pivotal piece in which he was able to successfully combine these seemingly opposite religious figures into one composition.

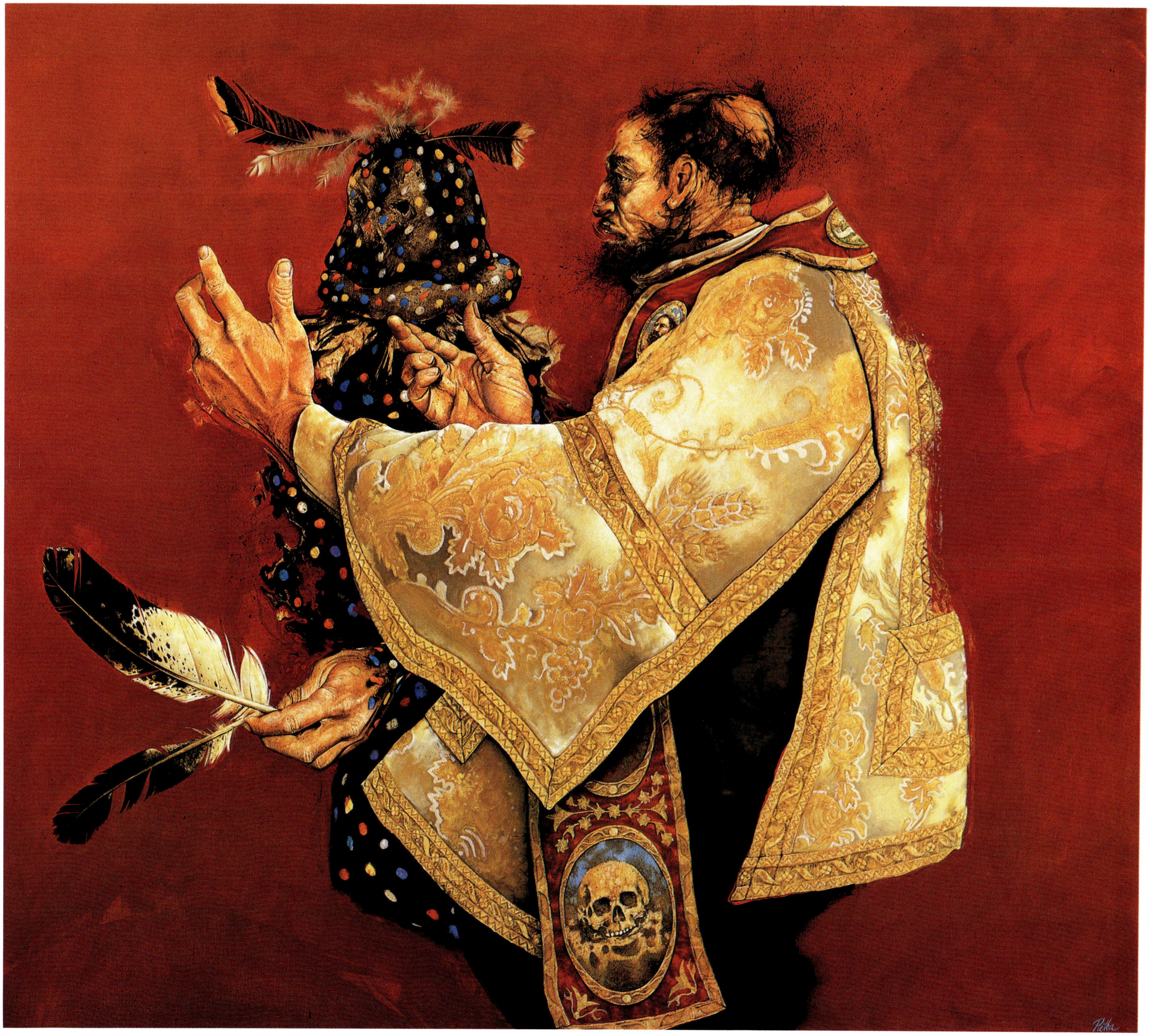

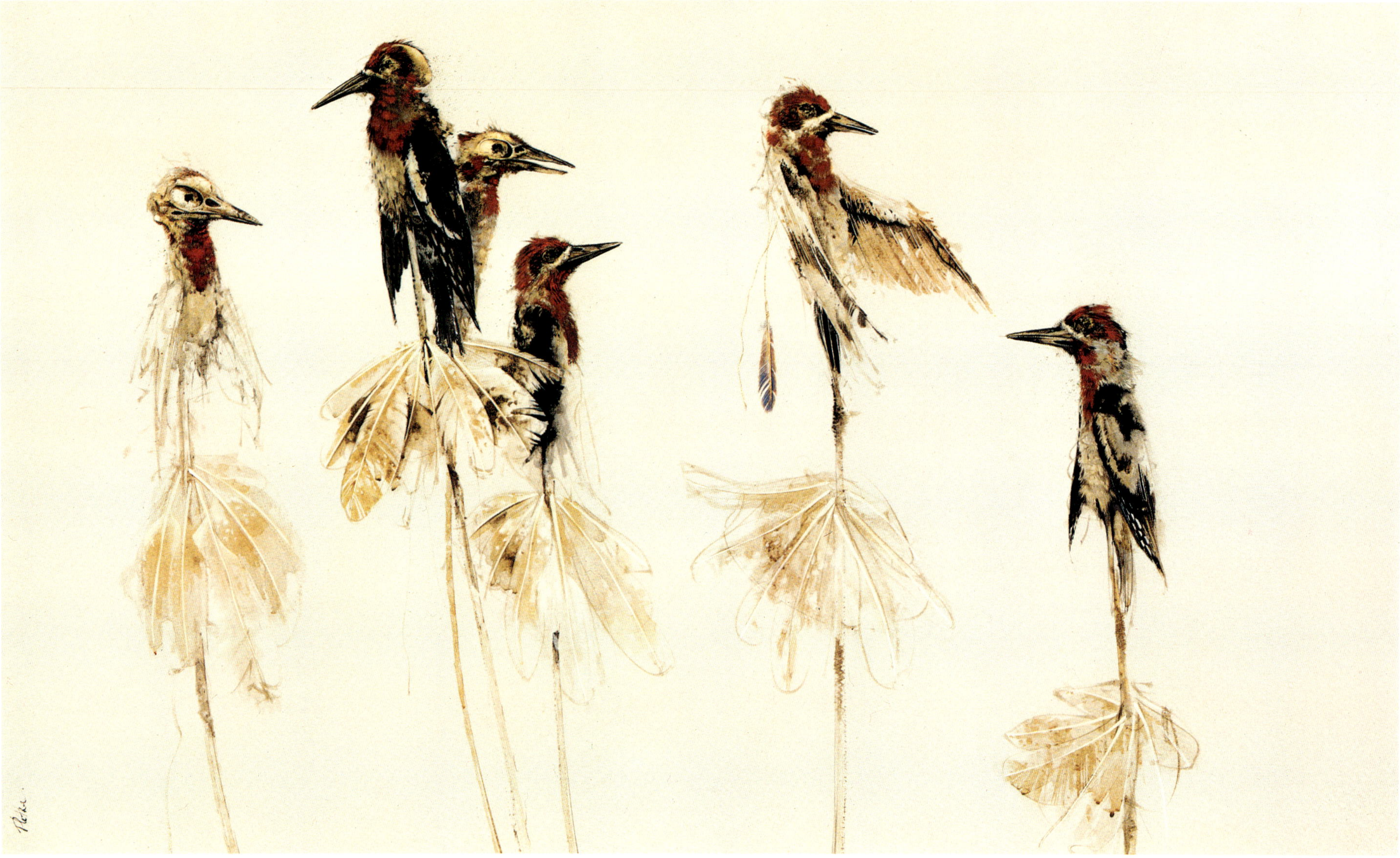

Ceremonial Bird Wands
1979
Acrylic on linen canvas
28 x 40

Pletka modeled this painting after a group of Hupa power wands he discovered in a museum in Arizona. The models consisted of woodpeckers stuffed with grass and impaled on sticks. Just below the birds were skirts of eagle-back feathers.

Slippery Eye
1979
Acrylic on linen canvas
60 x 42

Slippery Eye may be Pletka's best portrait to date. The Cree man's attire is based on a buffalo hide robe once owned by Mato-tope, second chief of the Mandans.

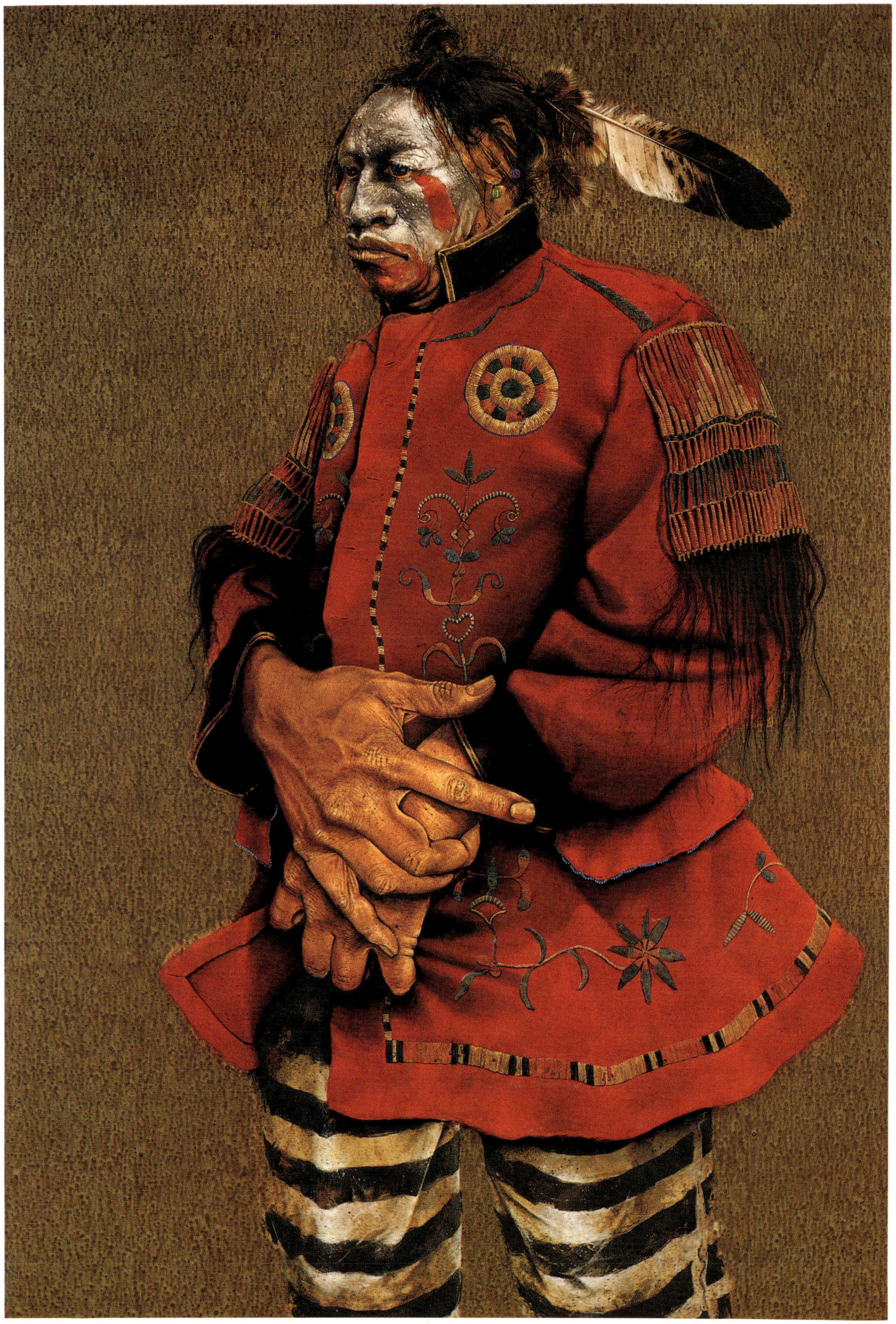

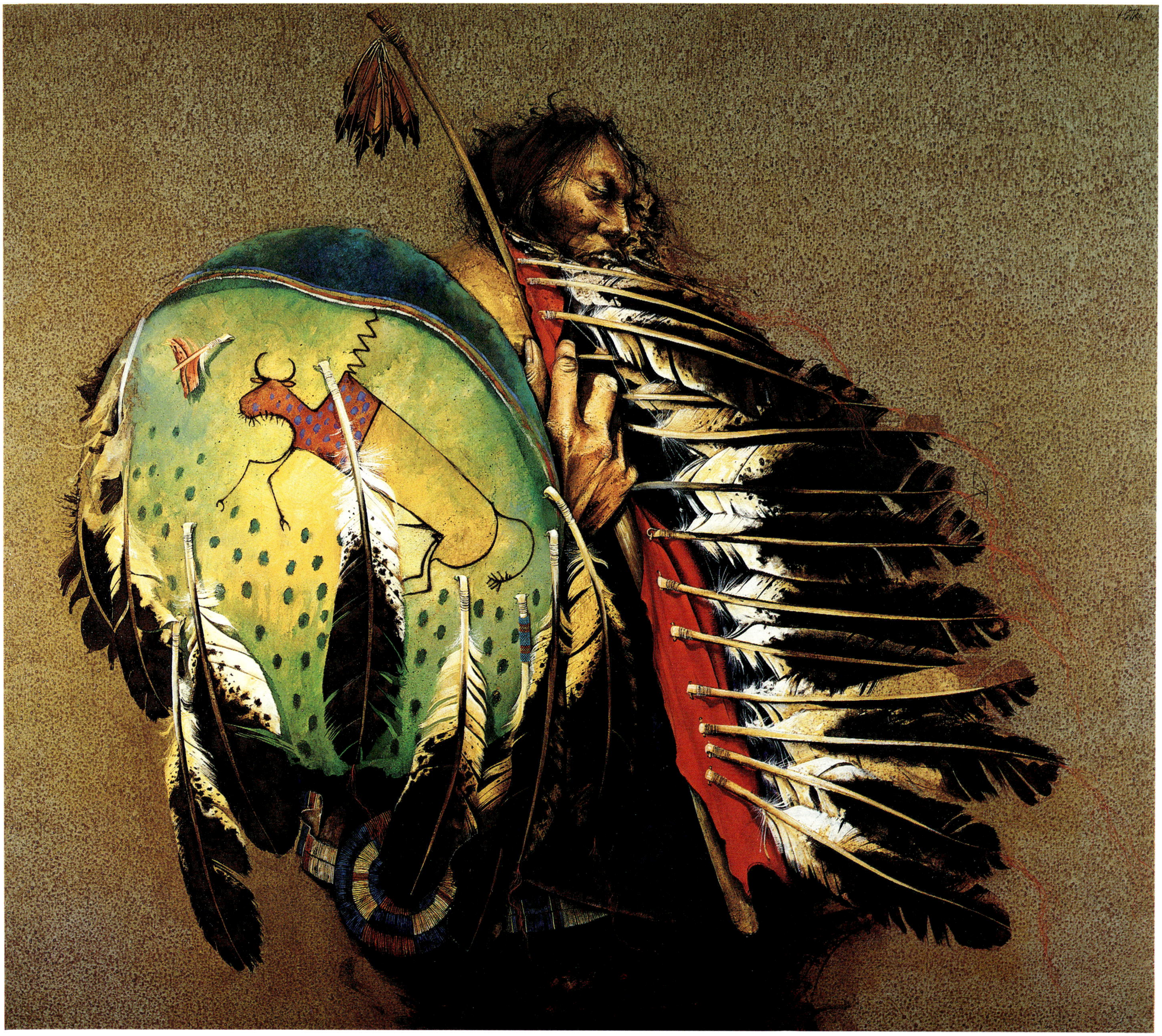

Rides the Whirlwind
1979
Acrylic on linen canvas
50 x 56

The fragmented face of this elderly Cheyenne warrior reveals a long life of anguish and sorrow. He fought resolutely duing the Indian Wars to save his buffalo hunting grounds, his sacred culture, and his lifestyle. But he lost. All he retains are memories of past glories and two symbols of his few brief triumphs—the society staff and society shield. Patterned after a museum piece, the shield depicts a buffalo connected by lightning and thunder to the dark clouds overhead.

Albino Deer Head
1979
Mixed media
30 x 18

The White Deer Dance was a renewal ceremony performed well into the 1900s by northern California tribes. Several of these, such as the Hupa, Tolowa, and Yurok, embraced wealth cults and caste systems based on affluence. Money took many forms: elaborate headdresses, shell skirts, strings of feathers, or albino deer skins, as depicted in this 1979 drawing.

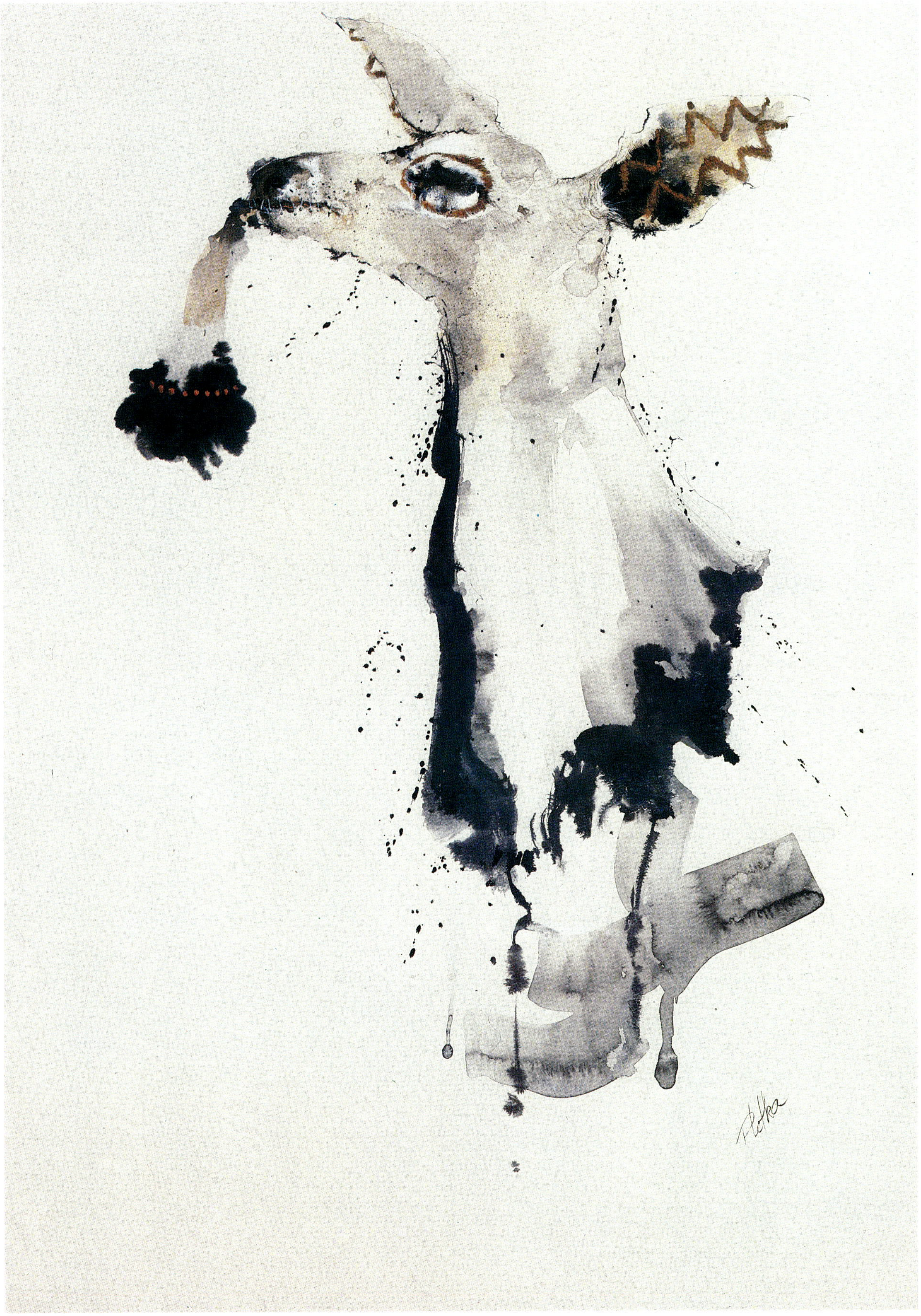

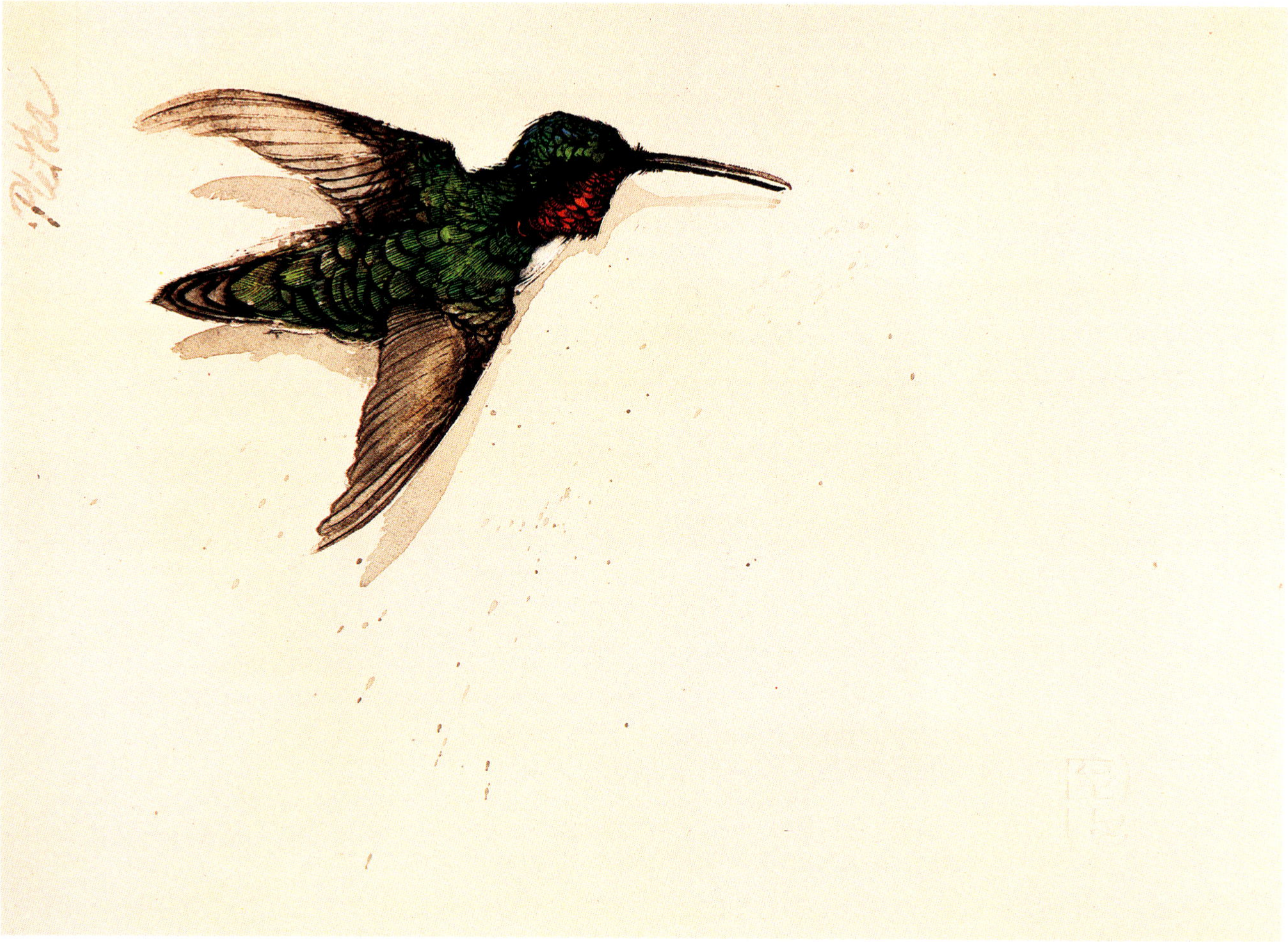

Ruby Throat
1979
Watercolor
5 x 7

The hummingbird has such a delicate metabolism that it must eat frequently to stay alive. It is particularly vulnerable if it hasn't eaten and the temperature suddenly drops. *Ruby Throat* is a watercolor of a little hummingbird found frozen after an unexpected cold snap.

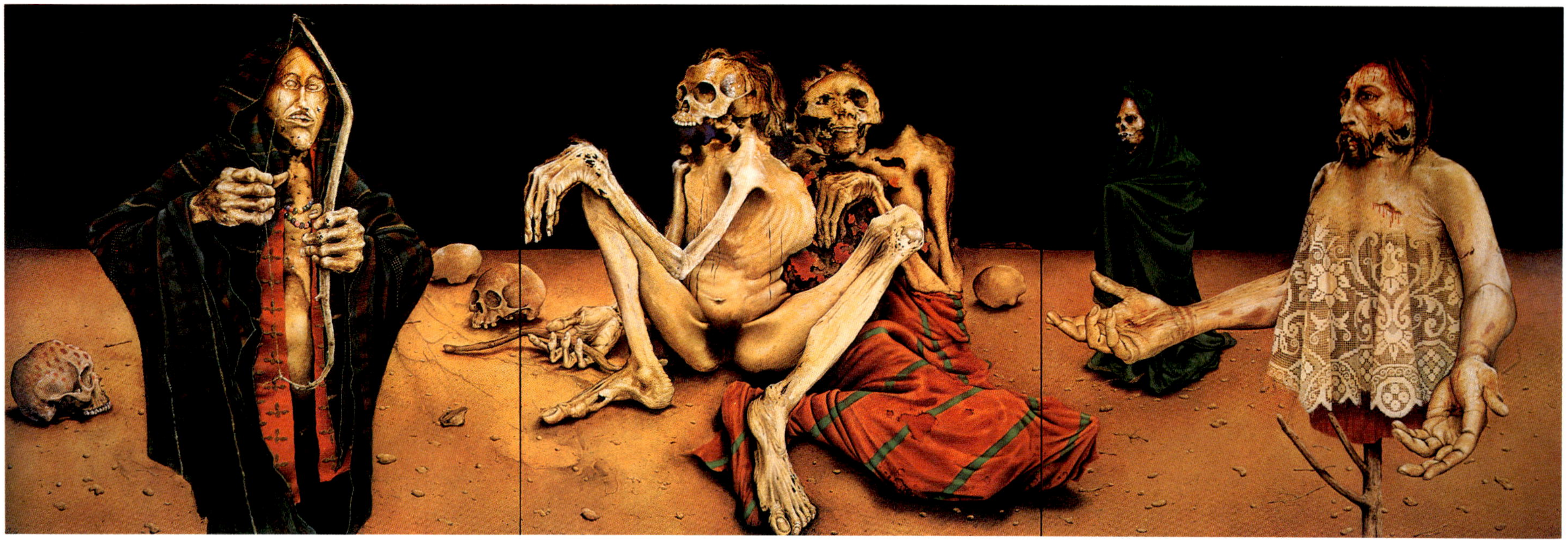

Las Muertas
1980
Acrylic on linen canvas
Triptych 48 x 144

No doubt Pletka's most controversial painting, *Las Muertas* is an allegorical portrayal of Penitente beliefs and ceremony. Three variations of the angel of death are depicted: the robed female figure carrying a bow with the long bullet-shaped mask, the female skeletal figure in the center with a misplaced lower jaw and snaggled teeth, and the small figure in green, representative of those carried in glass lanterns by children during the Lenten pilgrimage to the local calvary. The use of skulls is a reminder of the devotional religious carvings, or santos, found in many *moradas*. The skull with the red spots, however, and the mummy behind the seated female hint at a southwestern Indian flavor. Overall the painting is fraught with powerful and cryptic symbols of Christianity, most clearly defined by the inclusion of the Christ figure.

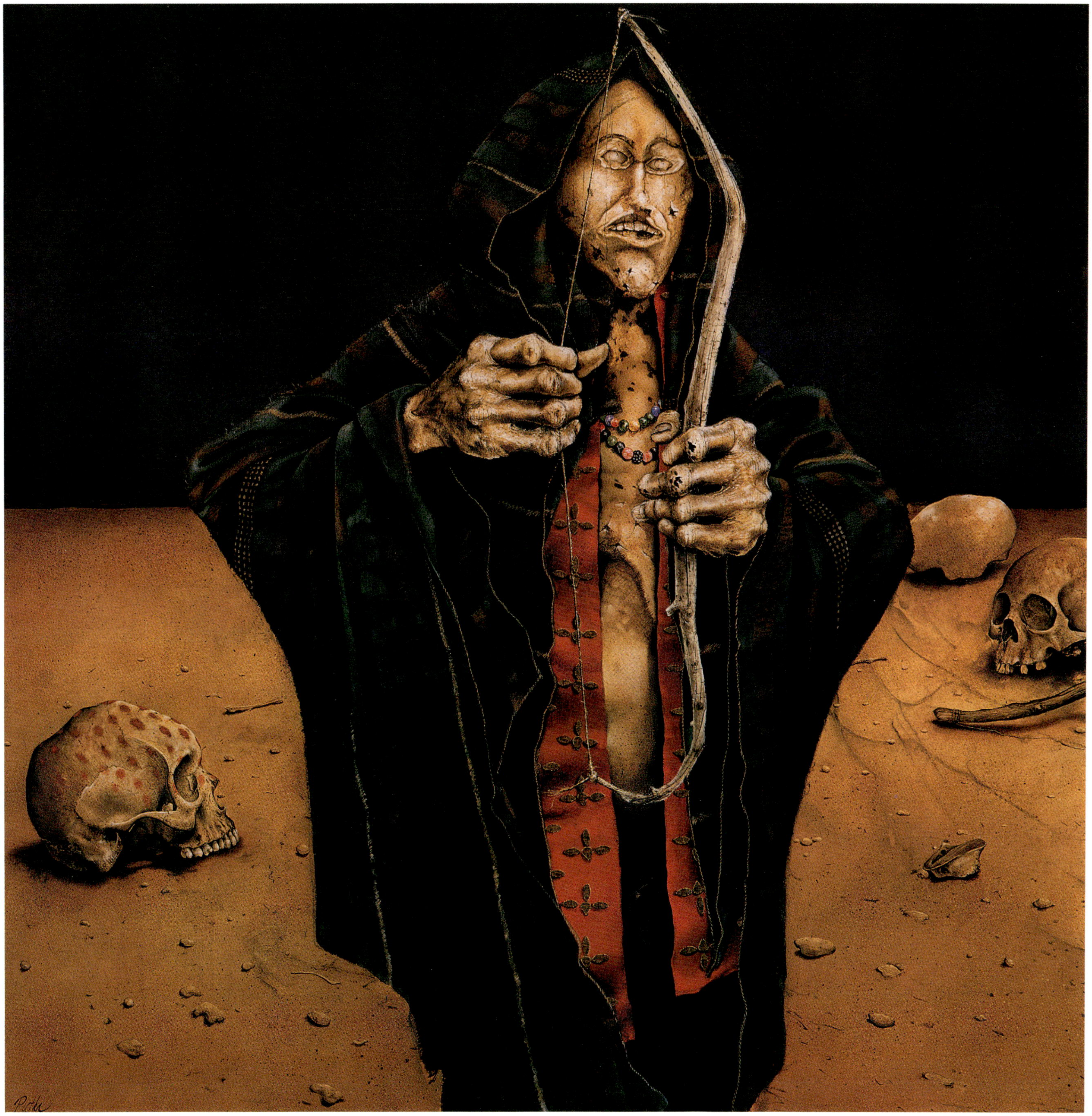

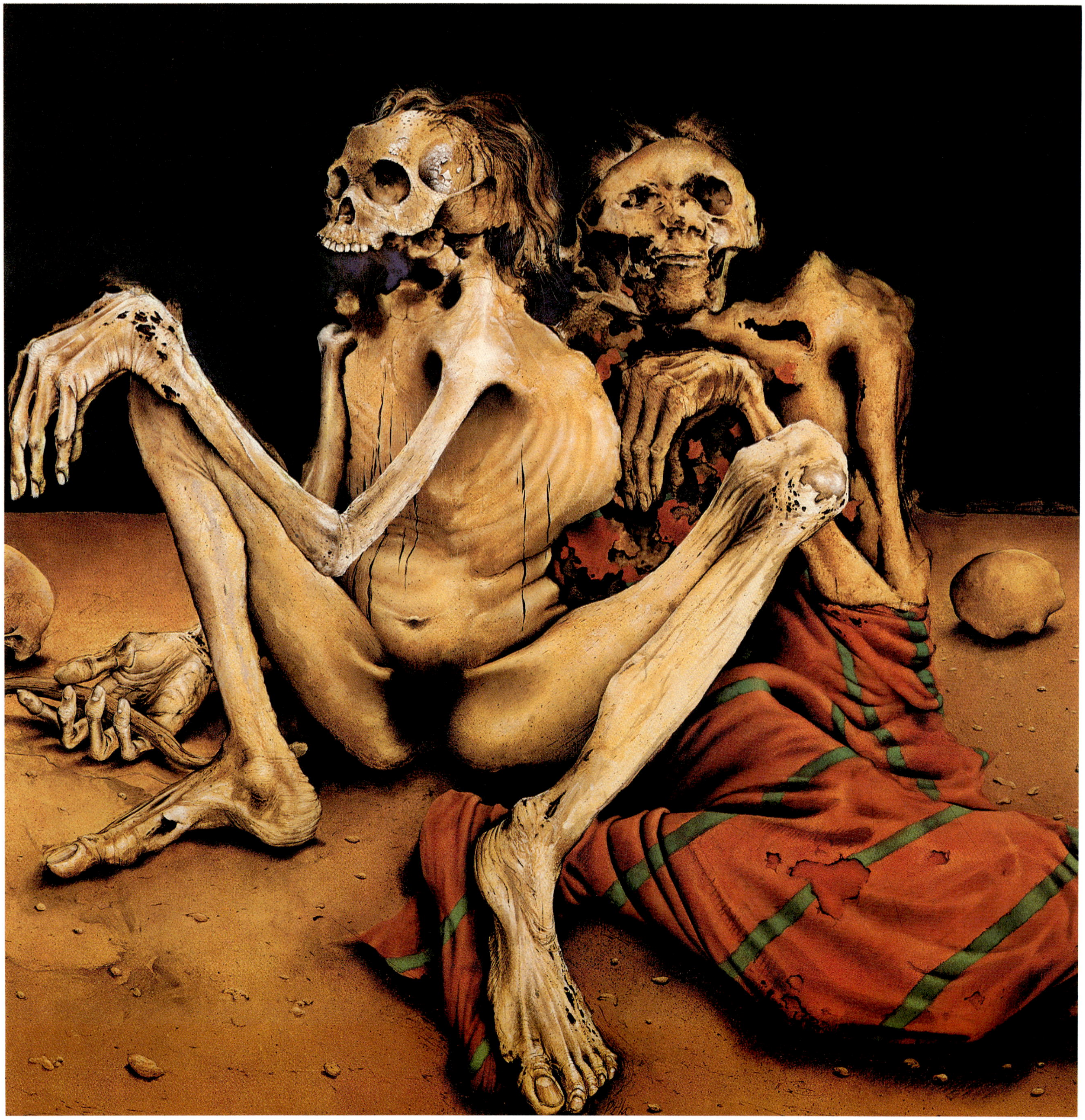

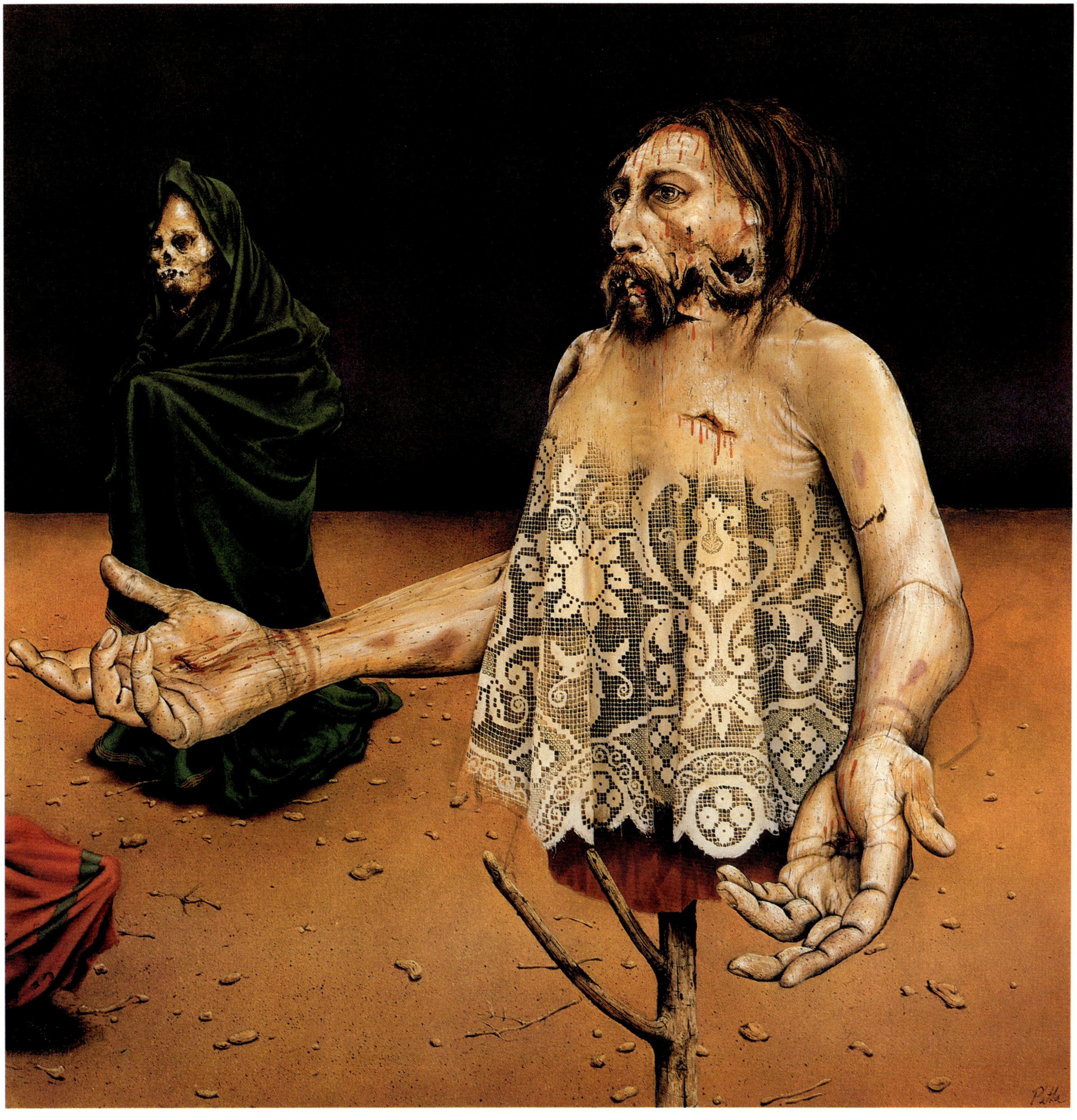

New Mexico Landscape
1980
Acrylic on linen canvas
52 x 60

This is the last painting Pletka did in 1980. The year was not particularly productive in terms of numbers, but he considers it his best year for growth and quality. *New Mexico Landscape* focuses on an enchanting environment and comments on Catholicism in the area. The crosses and the trees function as sculptures, as integral parts of the landscape. Among Penitentes, *desconsos* (resting places) ranged from crosses to little piles of rocks. The middle cross is patterned loosely after one that lies along the path of the procession to *Sanctuario de Chimayo,* where people visit each year at Easter time to gather some of the curative dirt kept in a hole in the ground inside the chapel. One cross was painted blue, a color locally believed to ward off witches. The one with spots was painted to suggest an Indian influence.

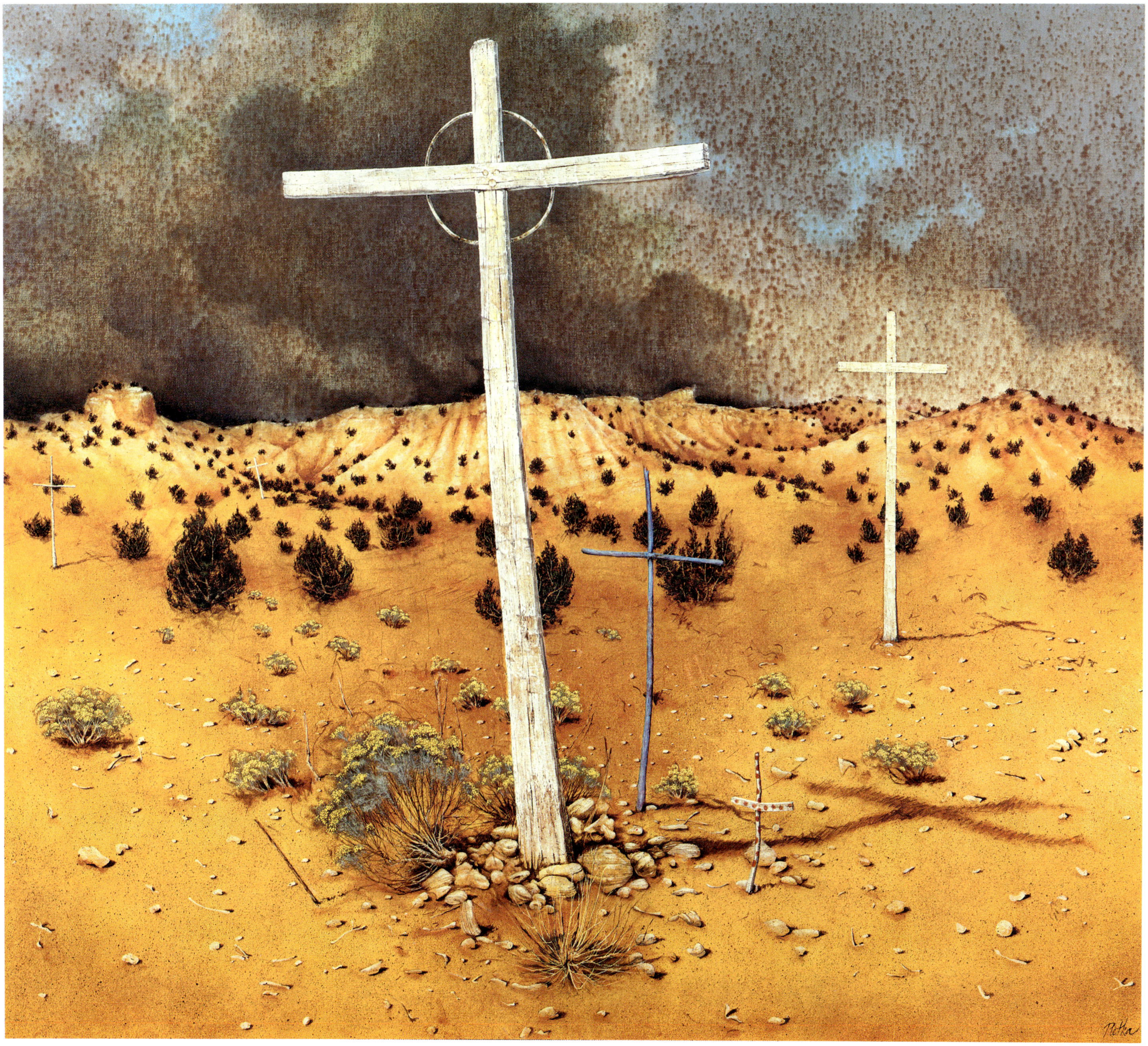

La Dona Sebastiana
1980
Acrylic on linen canvas
42 x 54

Simultaneously fascinating and foreboding, the *carreta de la muerte,* a Penitente invention, functions as a reminder of mortality. It is accepted that the first death cart was carved by Nasario Guadalupe Lopez (1821–1881) of Cordova, New Mexico. The piece was acquired by the Taylor Museum Collection of the Colorado Springs Fine Arts Center. Theories suggest the cart, typically bearing a female skeleton brandishing a bow and arrow, was based on the thirteenth Tarot card, depicting a skeleton with a scythe. Legend holds that strange clatter rising from the streets late at night is actually *La Dona Sebastiana* looking for her next victim. During Good Friday processions, the cart becomes a penance for Penitentes. Loaded with heavy stones, the cart with wheels that do not turn is dragged by the brothers, who are bound by flesh-gashing horsehair ropes. Inside, the wooden figure with straggling hair and a menacing stare holds the bow outstretched, with the arrow pulled taut and ready to indiscriminately strike with lethal force.

The Penitentes believe the cart implicity tells of the presence of death as a constant threat, but not a negative force. The existence of death makes life sweeter. When one realizes the confines of life, one appreciates life more—remembering that a judgment awaits.

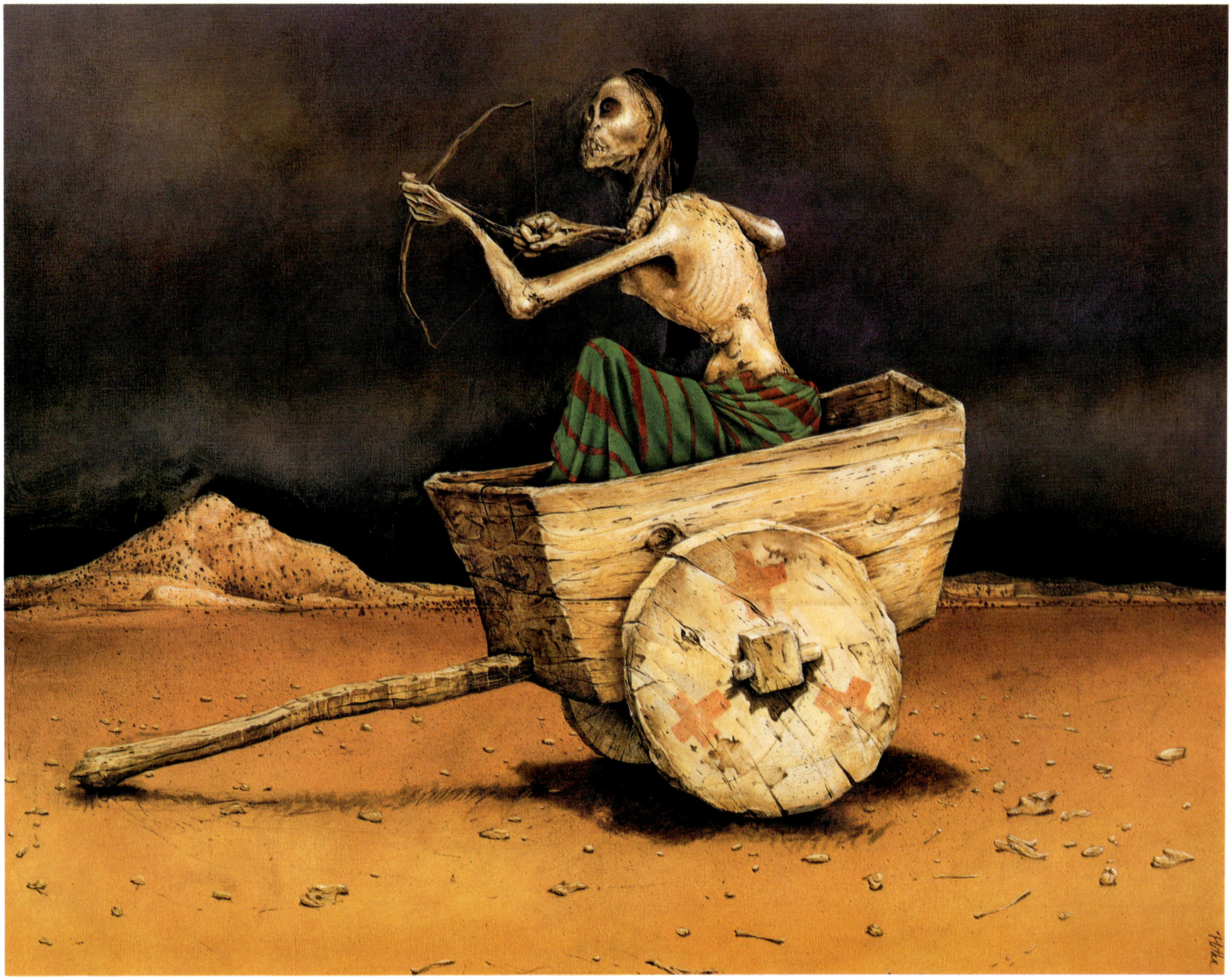

The Ceremony
1980
Acrylic on linen canvas
72 x 84

This man is in communion with the skulls of his ancestors and is, in an intense moment, beginning to switch identities with the red head directly in front of him. Pletka has trimmed the figure with a variety of artifacts, including a pair of moccasins drawn from his own collection. The quilled basket strip was researched from period pieces by Karl Bodmer.

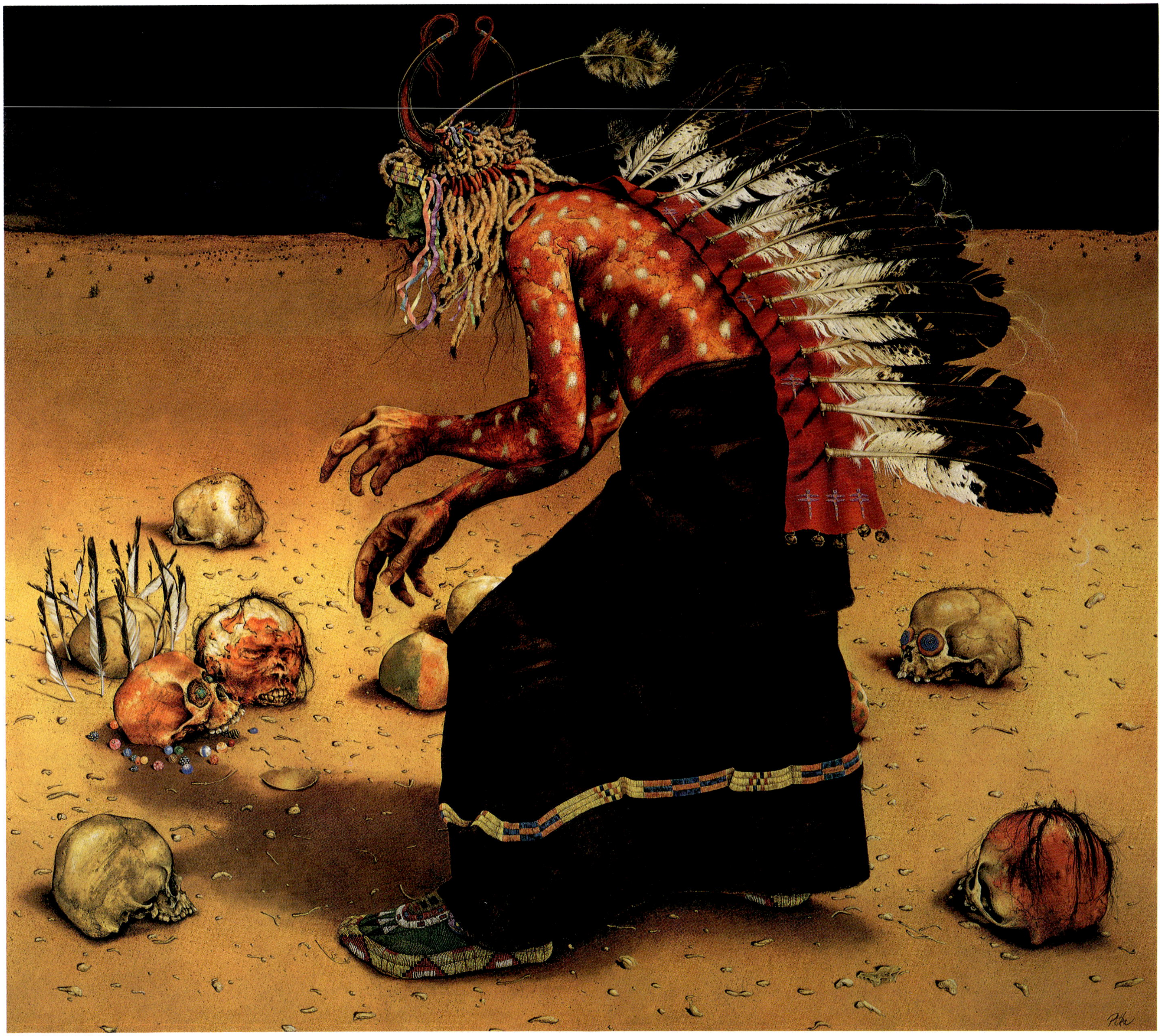

Dos Cabezas
1980
Watercolor
5 x 7

The image on the left is representative of the ancient funerary dolls included in Peruvian mummy bundles. Pletka conjectures that their purpose was similar to that of the Egyptian *ushabti*—"to help the dead once they've crossed the river." He, metaphorically, includes a skull in the composition.

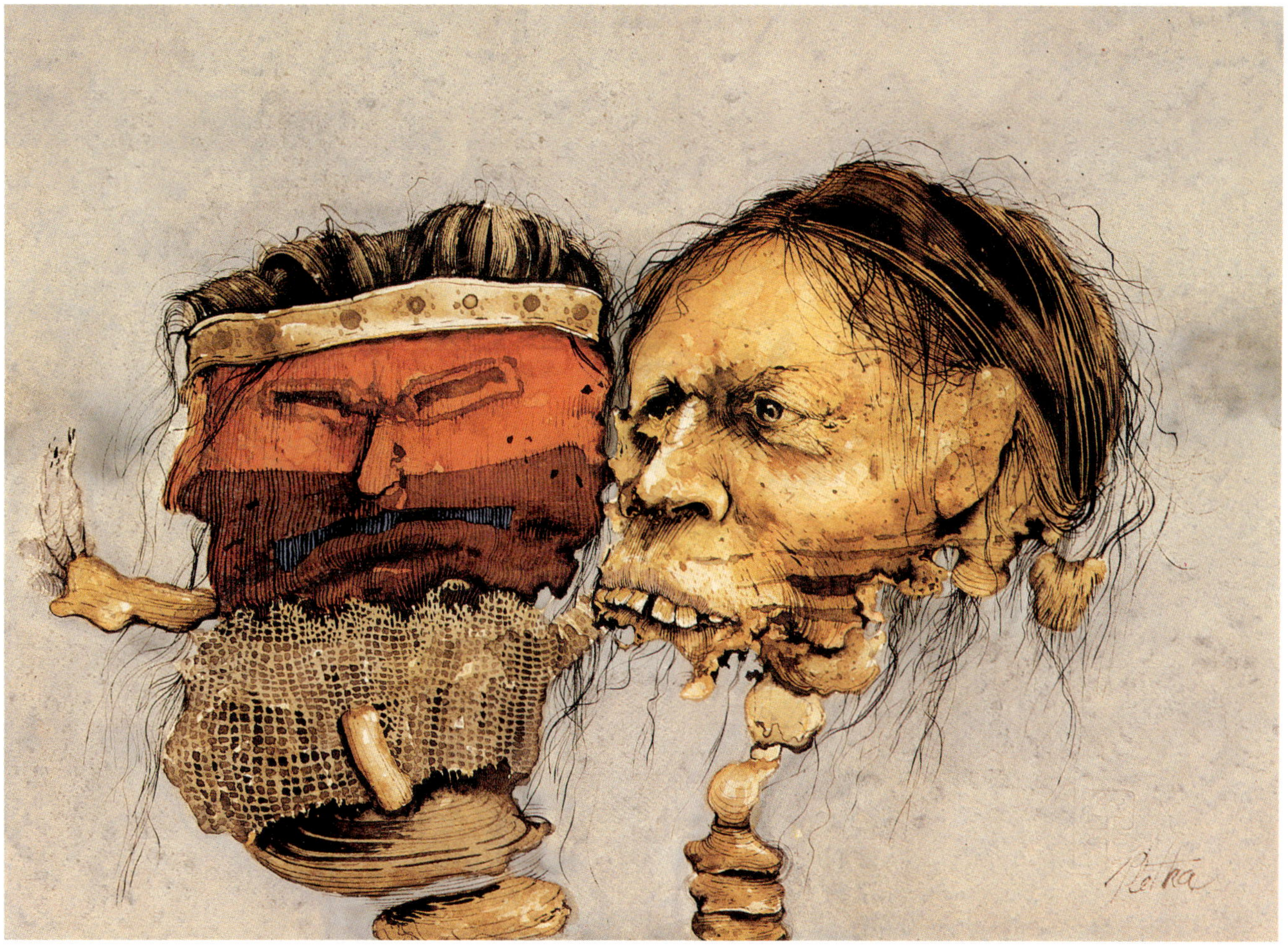

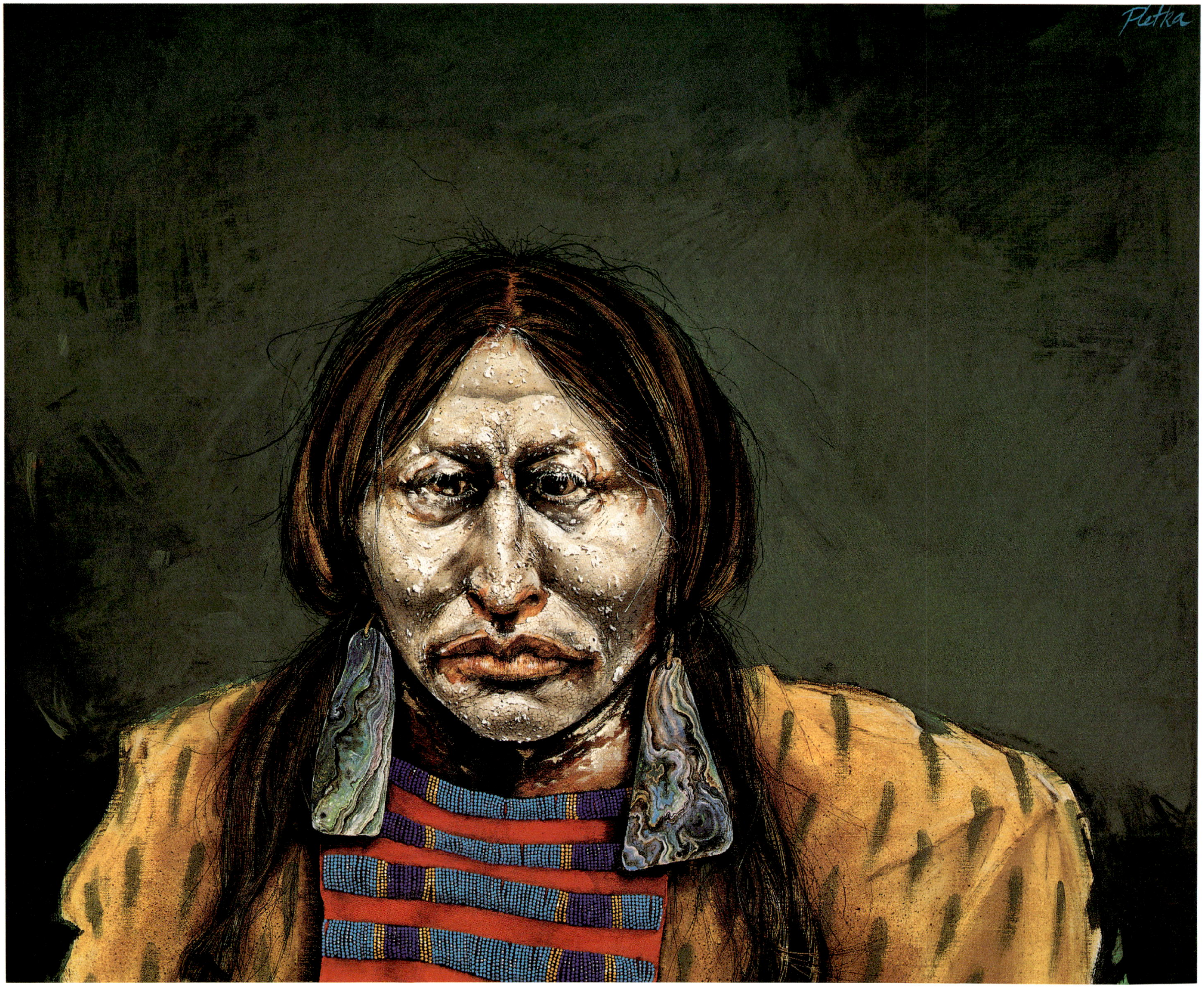
Pletka

White Faced Eagle
1981
Acrylic on linen canvas
26 x 34

This small portrait of a Cheyenne man, Pletka's last work in 1981, suggests a serenity and contentment reflective of the artist's feeling for the year's production.

Mesquaki
1981
Acrylic on linen canvas
66 x 50

Though his dress might suggest a sociable creature, *Mesquaki,* an Indian term for the Sauk and Fox tribe of Iowa, never got the chance to hobnob.

A note on the lining of the subject's coat, owned by Pletka, indicates it once belonged to a Civil War doctor. The epaulets, possibly of Indian manufacture, were added. He carries a Great Lake war club, wears a satin breechclout and trade bell earrings with ribbons. He has brownish hair and is balding slightly. Impacted by white culture and the interaction among tribes, many of the Indian's trappings were acquired through trade. His candy-striped face and legs indicate he is a scout for the U.S. Army.

It is an amazingly detailed painting. The cavalry coat buttons are complete to the last olive leaf and arrow.

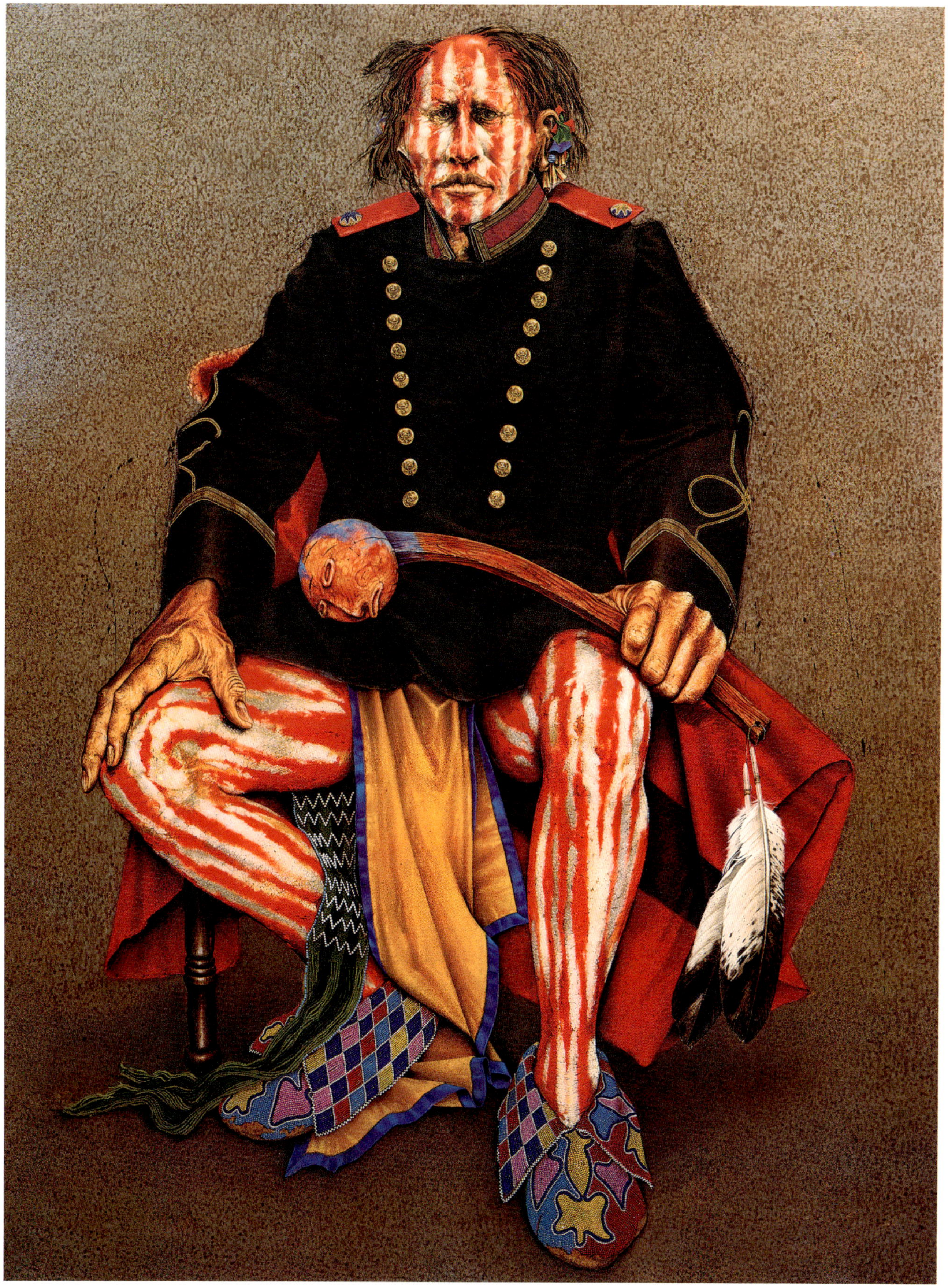

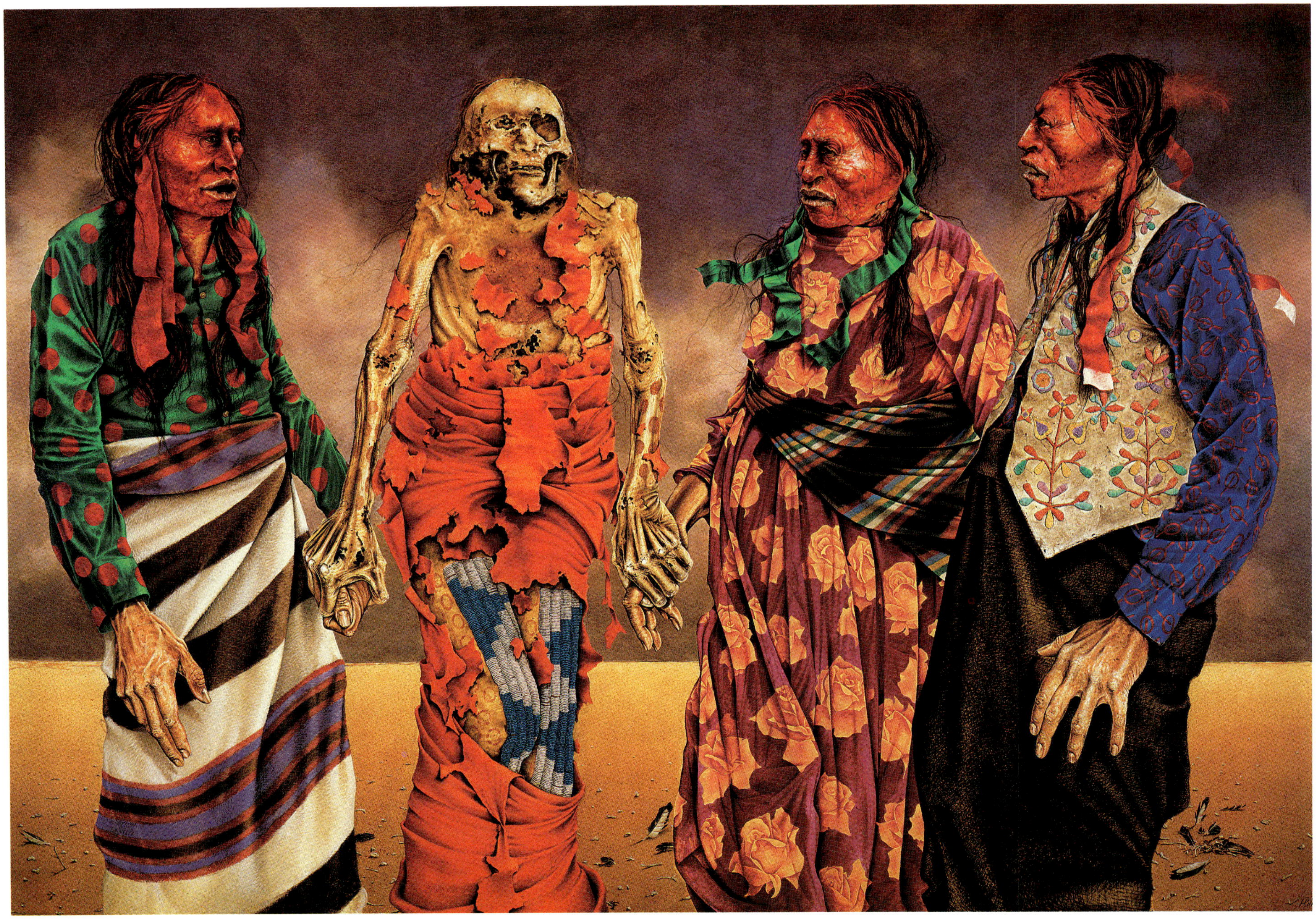

Wakan Dagre (God is Coming)
1981
Acrylic on linen canvas
72 x 108

The premise of the Ghost Dance was the revival of the old ways—to rid the land of the white men and bring back the buffalo. The dancers would chant and enter a trance during which they hoped to meet their relatives and bring them back to life. In the case of the Sioux Ghost Dance, two representatives, Kicking Bear and Short Bull, were sent from the Dakota reservation to Pyramid Lake in Nevada by railroad in search of Wovoka, the Paiute prophet who founded the religion. Wovoka, a Christian, envisioned a non-violent dance with no warlike attitudes, because only through peace could there be salvation. Short Bull and Kicking Bear brought news of the dance to the Sioux and incorporated some of the tribe's more aggressive attitudes into the dance.

The Ghost Dance participants in this painting are wearing the sacred red paint, as prescribed by Wovoka. They have brought back a member of the dead, but to no avail. Messengers who carried the Indians' prayers to God were battlefield birds, so many crows and magpies appear on the Ghost Dance shirts. What's left of a magpie is strewn on the ground, with a desolate landscape behind it. The woman wears a typical dress of the period. It looks like drapery material but is actually heavy printed cloth, a rose pattern. She wears a Mexican shawl around her middle. The man on the far right wears a quilled vest and a handmade cotton shirt. He has a red-dyed eagle breast feather in his hair, another Ghost Dance symbol. The man on the left wears a second phase Navajo chief blanket, very popular among Sioux then, and stroud braid wraps. The leggings on the corpse are old Plains type from the 1850s with blue and white pony beads and red circles painted against yellow-dyed buckskin. He's wrapped in a sacred red blanket.

Jicarilla
1981
Mixed media
30 x 30

The Jicarillas had an agency in Taos with the southern Utes. The chief was a Jicarilla; the agent was Kit Carson.

They were very fond of distinct bold patterns; accordingly, this sombre-looking man wears a special shirt adorned with a beaded triangular pattern. Black paint was daubed on the face to signify the success of a war party.

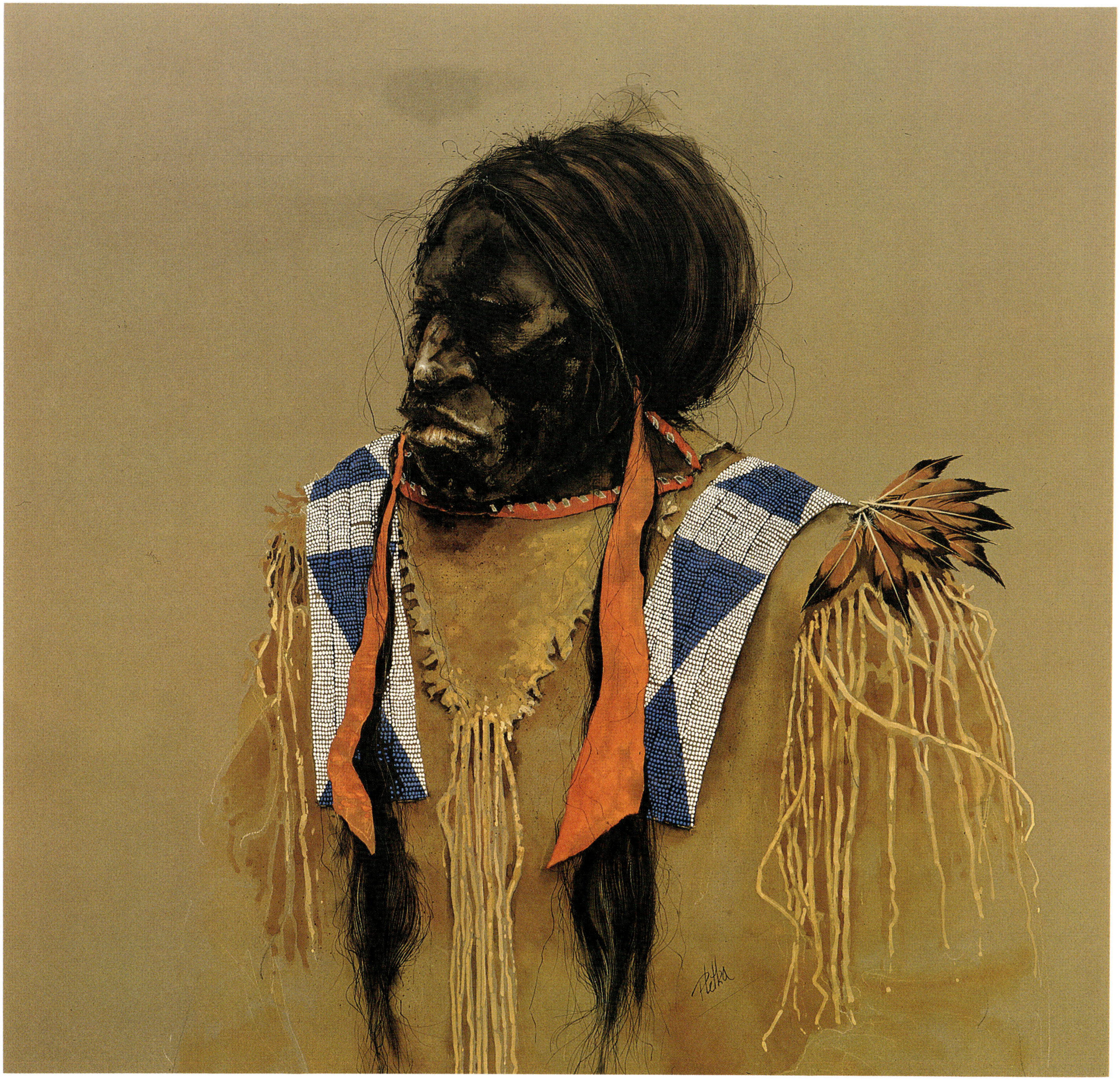

Tarahumara
1981
Acrylic on linen canvas
48 x 60

The Tarahumara Indians of the Sierra Madre Occidental in northern Mexico are a shy and peaceful group, who have combined their native rites with the Catholicism introduced by missionaries. This painting illustrates the Easter dance in which participants daub themselves with white paint, chant, and beat large drums made by Indian craftsmen. The dancer is imitating one of the Fariseos (Pharisees) who persecuted Jesus. The headdress is an ordinary straw hat wrapped with a red bandana and stuffed with turkey tail and wing feathers. A long, red stroud trails behind. He also wears a sash and old pin-striped trousers. The bag he carries on his back holds his regular clothing.

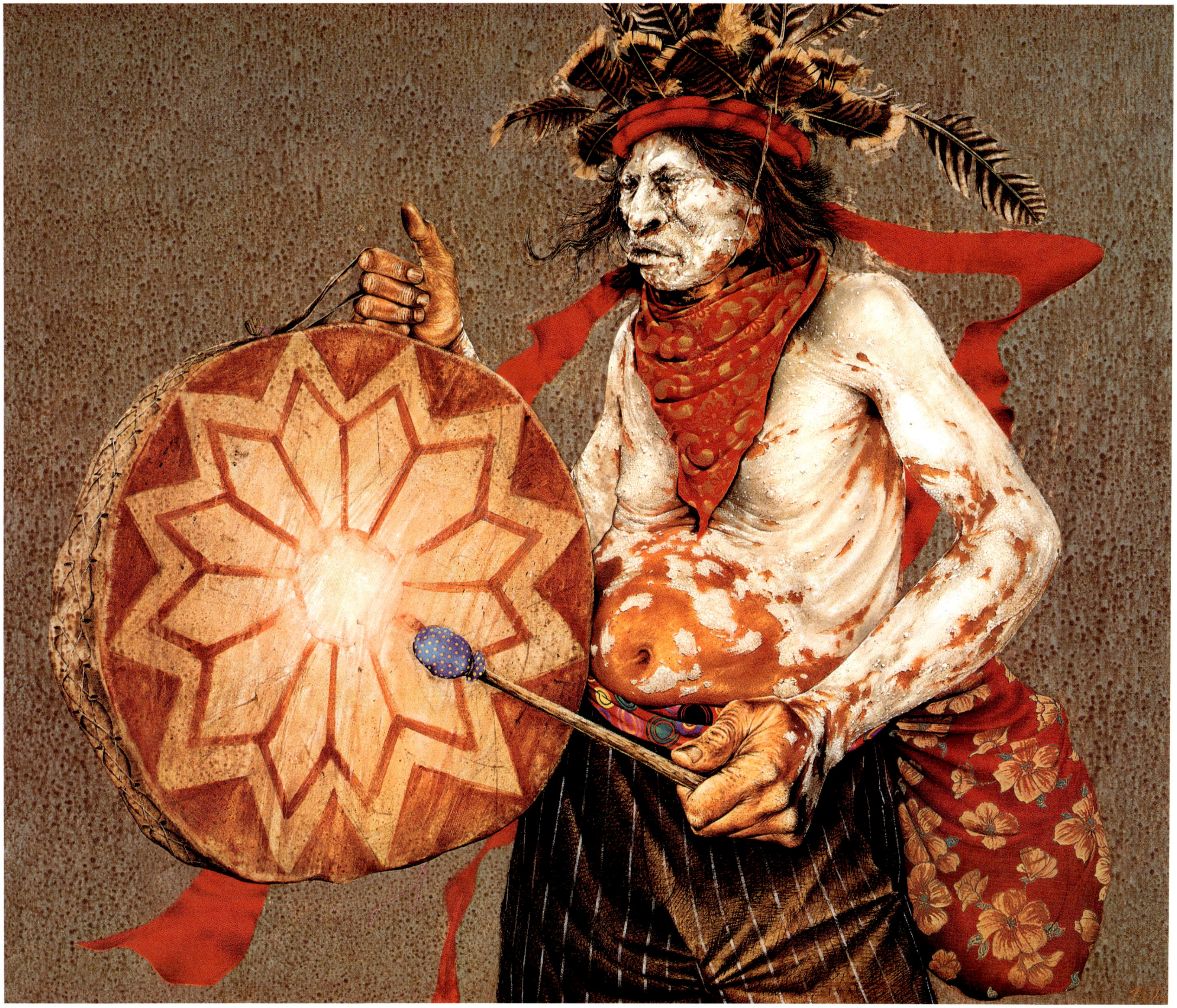

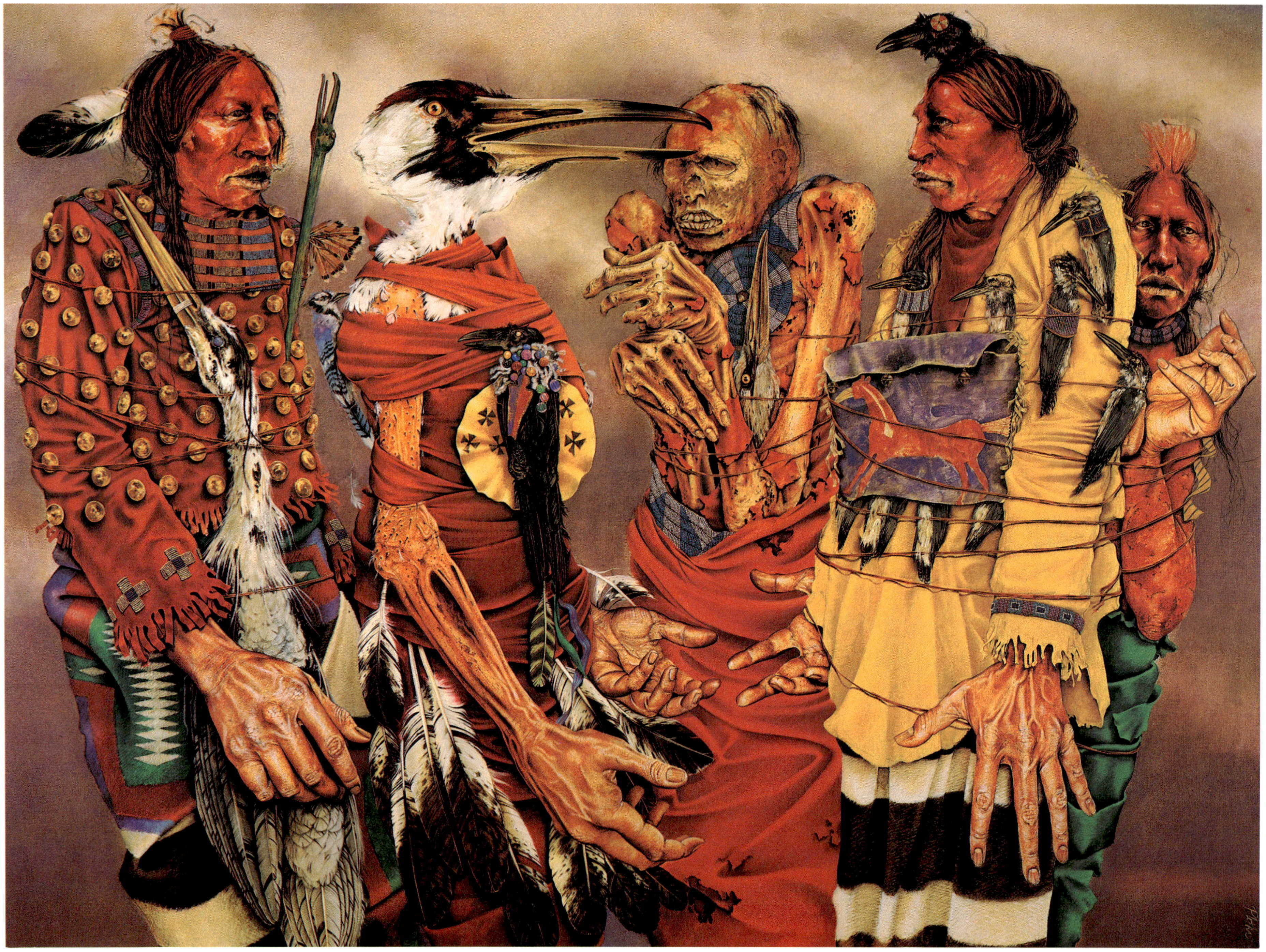

The Bonds of Antiquity
1982
Acrylic on linen canvas
60 x 82

This provocative painting consummates the use of symbols and talismans so significant to Pletka's earlier work.

The man on the left wears a war shirt, as distinguished from the "old man" shirts commonly called war shirts. The talisman flute, wedged under his arm, serves as a counterpart to the real heron tied to the fetish. The man metamorphosed into a whooping crane is bound by "list cloth"; appended is a small medicine shield. Bulletproofing kingfishers ring the individual on the right who sports a medicine parfleche.

Concomitance

Acknowledgments

Our pleasure in publishing a book of this magnitude has been heightened by the opportunity to share portions of the experience with several very sophisticated and knowledgeable people and organizations. Included in this group are the many Pletka admirers and collectors who have so generously shared their recollections and perspectives.

The contributions of Edna Gundersen and Nancy and Paul Pletka, in the preparation of this book, are also gratefully acknowledged.

Our deep appreciation is extended to the Jack O'Grady Galleries; to the InterNorth Art Foundation, Joslyn Art Museum, Omaha, Nebraska, for granting permission to reproduce "A Bison Painted Robe" by Karl Bodmer; to The Art Institute of Chicago for making available for our use "The Picture of Dorian Gray" by Ivan Le Lorraine Albright; and to Editions Gallimard, Paris, France, for its contribution.

PHOTOGRAPHIC CREDITS

Cradoc-Bagshaw, Vince Foster, Ted Hill, Jerry Jacka, Ray Manley, Tom McDonald, Bill Mclemore, Robert Nugent, Robert Reck, John Youngblut

Reading List

Primitive Cultures: North and South American Indians

The American Indian—The American Flag. Flint, Michigan: Flint Institute of Art, 1975.

Berlandier, Jean-Louis. *The Indians of Texas in 1830.* Washington, D.C.: Smithsonian Institution Press, 1969.

Catlin, George. *Letters and Notes on the Manners, Customs, and Conditions of North American Indians.* New York: Dover Publications, 1973.

Coe, Ralph T. *Sacred Circles.* London: Arts Council of Great Britain, 1965.

Denig, Edwin Thomson. *Five Indian Tribes of the Upper Missouri.* Norman: University of Oklahoma Press, 1961.

Ewers, John C. *Indian Life on the Upper Missouri.* Norman: University of Oklahoma Press, 1961.

Feder, Norman. *American Indian Art.* New York: Abrams, 1965.

———. *American Indian Art Before 1850.* Denver, Colorado: Denver Art Museum, 1965.

Fontana, Bernard and Schafer, John P. *Tarahumara.* Flagstaff, Arizona: Northland Press, 1979.

Frank, Larry and Harlow, Francis H. *Historic Pottery of the Pueblo Indians.* Boston: New York Graphic Society, Ltd., 1975.

Grinnell, George Bird. *Cheyenne Indians,* v. 1–2. Lincoln: University of Nebraska Press, 1972.

Hartmann, Horst. *Die Plains und Prairieindianer Nordeamerikas.* Berlin: Museum für Völkerkunde, 1979.

I Wear the Morning Star. Minneapolis: Minneapolis Institute of Art, 1976.

La Barre, Weston. *The Ghost Dance.* New York: Dell Publishing Co., Inc., 1970.

Lapiner, Alan. *Pre-Columbian Art of South America.* New York: Abrams, 1976.

Maurer, Evan. *The Native American Heritage.* Chicago: The Art Institute of Chicago, 1977.

Minneapolis Institute of Art, Walker Art Center/Indian Art Association. *American Indian Art: Form and Tradition.* New York: E. P. Dutton & Co., 1972.

Mooney, James. *The Ghost-Dance Religion and the Sioux Outbreak of 1890.* Chicago: University of Chicago Press, 1965.

Newton, Douglas. *Masterpieces of Primitive Art: The Nelson A. Rockefeller Collection.* New York: Alfred A. Knopf, 1978.

Powell, Peter. *People of the Sacred Mountain,* v. 1–2. New York: Harper & Row, 1981.

Scherer, Joanna Cohan. *Indians.* New York: Crown Publishers, 1973.

Thomas, Davis and Ronnefeldt, Karin, eds. *People of the First Man.* New York: E. P. Dutton, 1976.

Wildschut, William. *Crow Indian Medicine Bundles.* New York: New York Museum of the American Indian, Heye Foundation, 1975.

Wormington, H. M. *Ancient Man in North America.* Denver, Colorado: The Denver Museum of Natural History, 1957.

Penitentes/Hispanic

Boyd, E. *Popular Arts of Spanish New Mexico.* Santa Fe: Museum of New Mexico Press, 1974.

Darlex, Alex. *The Passionists.* Glorieta, New Mexico: Rio Grande Press, 1968.

Horka-Follick, Lorayane Ann. *Los Hermanos Penitentes.* Los Angeles: Westernlore Press, 1969.

Santos of the Southwest. Denver, Colorado: Denver Art Museum.

Weigle, Marta. *Brothers of Light, Brothers of Blood.* Albuquerque: University of New Mexico Press, 1976.

General Art

Bauer, John, ed. *New Art in America.* Greenwich, Connecticut: New York Graphic Society, 1957.

Boswell, Payton. *Modern American Painting.* New York: Dodd, Mead & Co., 1939.

De Tolnay, Charles. *Hieronymus Bosch.* New York: Reynal & Co., 1966.

Janson, H. W. *History of Art.* New York: Abrams Press, 1977.

Klein, Mina and Arthur. *Käthe Kollwitz: Life in Art.* New York: Schocken Books, 1976.

Swaan, Wim. *The Late Middle Ages.* Ithaca, New York: Cornell University Press, 1977.

Trucchi, Lorenza. *Francis Bacon.* New York: Abrams, 1975.

Art Index

*© Jack O'Grady Galleries

DESIGNED BY MICHAEL HOLLAR
COMPOSED IN PHOTOTYPE BEMBO WITH
DISPLAY LINES IN EGYPTIAN SURROUNDED
PRINTED ON QUINTESSENCE DULL

PUBLISHED BY THE PRESS IN THE PINES

NORTHLAND PRESS